To Haley & Joey,

Have fun with this one!

Love   Baba & Nana

VeggieTales
BIBLE MANIA

by Cindy Kenney

www.bigidea.com

INTEGRITY®
PUBLISHERS
family

www.integritypublishers.com

VeggieTales Bible Mania

Copyright © 2006 by Big Idea, Inc.
Illustrations copyright © 2006 by Big Idea, Inc.

Requests for information should be addressed to:
Integrity Publishing, 5250 Virginia Way, Suite 110, Brentwood, TN 37027

———————————————

Written by: Cindy Kenney
Research by: Rhonda Hogan, Cindy Kenney, Ron Eddy, and Karen Poth
Art Direction: John Trent
Layout and Design: John Trent and Cheryl Blum

Unless otherwise noted, scripture quotations are taken from the HOLY BIBLE, NEW INTERNATIONAL VERSION ® Copyright © 1973, 1978, 1984 by International Bible Society. Used by permission of Zondervan Publishing House. All rights reserved. Additional scripture quotations are taken from The King James Version (KJV). Public domain.

VeggieTales®, character names, likenesses and other indicia are trademarks of Big Idea, Inc. All rights reserved. Used under license.

ISBN 10:1-59145-434-4
ISBN 13:978:1-59145-434-2

Printed in the United States of America

06 07 08 09 QBR 9 8 7 6 5 4 3 2 1

TABLE OF CONTENTS

CONTENTS (CONT.)

INTRODUCTION

All Scripture is God-breathed and is useful for teaching, rebuking, correcting and training in righteousness, so that the man of God may be thoroughly equipped for every good work (2 Timothy 3:16–17).

THE BIBLE is packed full of truth—stories and wisdom relevant to all of us today. As Scripture tells us, it is God's Word! Through the Bible, God teaches us how to live godly lives, deal with everyday problems, live fully despite tough questions, and learn who God is and what he is doing.

The Bible reveals how God works in our world. We read about the faith journey of the Israelites in the Old Testament. Then the New Testament provides us with the accounts of Jesus's life, death, and resurrection. The four Gospels are followed by stories of early Christians, the start of the church, and further wisdom for how to love God and our neighbor.

You can read the same passage of Scripture at different times in your life, and at each reading, you can receive more understanding from it. That's because God works through the Scriptures! The Bible is God's amazing communication source that he allows us to use every day of our lives!

So why a *VeggieTales Bible Mania* book? Big Idea and Integrity Publishers want to make opening the Bible a fun experience that bears fruit. We're all about teaching kids important values from the Bible—so why not help kids find fun new ways to learn amazing facts, figures, stories, and wisdom from Scripture? To add to the fun, you'll even find some interesting Veggie information along the way.

Go ahead—turn the page and get started! Join Bob, Larry, and the rest of your favorite Veggie characters as they explore the most important book of all time . . . the Bible!

IN THE BEGINNING . . .

In the beginning, God created the heavens and the earth (Genesis 1:1).

What existed at the very beginning of time? Nothing . . . except God!

God made the world in six amazing days! Can you name what God did on each day of Creation?

Day 1: God made light and dark.
Day 2: God made the waters and the sky.
Day 3: God made dry land and plants.
Day 4: God made the sun, moon, and stars.
Day 5: God made the fish and birds.
Day 6: God made animals and man.
Day 7: God rested!

• How big is the universe? We can't even begin to see the end of the universe by looking up at the sky. Scientists have tried to measure distances between planets and stars to give us some idea of how big it is. The farthest object that they have found is 17,000 million light years away from earth.

• What is the Milky Way? It is the galaxy which is the home of our solar system.

• How many stars are in the Milky Way? Astronomers estimate that there are about 100-200 billion stars in our galaxy.

• Which planets do not have any moons? Both Mercury and Venus do not have any moons.

- How many moons are there orbiting the planet Jupiter? Jupiter is like a mini solar system with sixty-three moons! The fifth planet outward from the sun, and the largest planet in our solar system, has a moon called Ganymede with a diameter of 3,273 miles. This moon is larger than Mercury and Pluto!

- How long does it take the earth to travel around the sun? It takes one *day* for the earth to rotate once on its axis. It takes one *month* for the moon to change from new to full and back again. It takes one *year* for the earth to revolve around the sun.

Veggie Fun!

In another beginning ... VeggieTales was created!

In 1966, in Muscatine, Iowa, a quiet boy was born. Silly things kept popping into his head that managed to get him in trouble at Sunday school. His name was Phil Vischer.

A Tomato and Cucumber Are Born!

As Phil got older, he noticed that the values he learned in the Bible didn't line up with the values in movies or on TV. So Phil paired up with a pal from Bible college, named Mike Nawrocki, and they decided to do something about it.

Though no one knew it at the time, Bob the Tomato had just met Larry the Cucumber. Three years later, they began work on the first VeggieTales story: *Where's God When I'm S-Scared?*

GOD CREATED THE LAND AND SEA

And God said, "Let there be an expanse between the waters to separate water from water" (Genesis 1:6).

God created large areas of land that we call continents. Today, the seven continents have been divided into smaller areas called countries, cities, towns, farmlands, deserts, mountains, and villages.

- Where did the first four rivers originate? The Garden of Eden. What are their names? Pishon, Gihon, Tigris, and Euphrates.

- What are the two longest rivers in the world? 1. The Nile, located in Egypt, is approximately 4,132 miles long. 2. The Amazon, located in South America, is approximately 4,000 miles long. At certain times of the year, the rainfall actually causes the Nile to be longer than the Amazon.

- What are the two areas of lowest elevation on earth? 1. On dry land, the Dead Sea which is located between Jordan and Israel, is over 1,200 feet below sea level! The Dead Sea is so salty that animals and fish cannot even live in it! In the Bible, it is known by other names like the Salt Sea *(Numbers 34:12)* or the Eastern Sea *(Joel 2:18-20)*. 2. In the ocean, the deepest part is in the Pacific Ocean near Japan. It is called Challenger Deep and is approximately 36,000 feet deep.

- What's the largest desert in the world? The Sahara, in North Africa, spans an area nearly 3.5 million square miles! The lower forty-eight states of the United States could fit into that area.

- What is the biggest lake? The Caspian Sea in Europe and Asia is approximately 143,000 square miles.

- What is the biggest lake in the United States? Lake Superior is 31,700 square miles. What is the highest waterfall in the world? Angel Falls in Venezuela is 3,212 feet tall!

- What is the highest mountain? Mt. Everest is 29,035 feet above sea level.

- Did you know that volcanoes are mentioned in the Bible? See *Psalm 104:31–32.*

- How tall were the Bible mountains?
- Mount Ararat: 16,900 ft.
- Mount of Olives: 2,690 ft.
- Mount Lebanon: 10,000 ft.
- Mount Zion: 2,533 ft.
- Mount Sinai: 7,500 ft.
- Mount of Jesus's Temptation: 1,148 ft.

Storm from *Jonah—a VeggieTales Movie*

Some Veggies Went to Sea, Sea, Sea to See What They Could See, See, See . . .

- Name the five Veggie characters who were marooned at sea during their three-hour tour. Bob the Tomato—the skipper; Larry the Cucumber—the skipper's little buddy; Dad Asparagus—the professor; Archibald Asparagus—the millionaire; Lovey Asparagus —the millionaire's wife.

- In *The Search for Samson's Hairbrush*, did Minnesota Cuke travel to a dessert or an island? It was the Island of Malta. (Malta is an island, a Malt is a dessert.)

- What three VeggieTales shows had terrible storms at sea? *Jonah—a VeggieTales Movie*™; *Lyle the Kindly Viking*; and *Larry's Lagoon* from *God Wants Me to Forgive Them*?

9

GOD CREATED THE EARTH AND SKY

God made two great lights — the greater light to govern the day and the lesser light to govern the night. He also made the stars (Genesis 1:16).

Fun Space Facts

When God created the earth, he protected it with a huge blanket of gases that we call the atmosphere. The atmosphere fades into space about 180 miles above the earth. We call it the sky.

Did you know that . . .

- when you enjoy the daylight sun, it's nighttime for people on the other side of the earth?

- on a cloudy day, the sun is still shining? You just can't see it, because it's hidden by the clouds.

- the only time it's dark during the day is when the moon blocks the sun? That's called a total eclipse, which only lasts for a few minutes.

- there is only one star that can make us sunburned? That star is called our sun, which is 109 times the size of Earth.

- we can't really measure the size of the universe? Scientists have tried to measure the distance between the stars and planets. That's called a light year (the speed that light travels in one year). The farthest object that we know about is a star that is 17,000 million light years away. David wrote about the sky and heavens in Psalm 19:1–4.

- Can you name the nine different planets in our solar system that move around the sun along a path called an orbit? They are Mercury, Venus, Earth, Mars, Jupiter, Saturn, Uranus, Neptune, and Pluto. But there are thousands of different solar systems in our galaxy that God created! It is believed that there may be over 100 billion galaxies. God was really busy!

- What holds together all the billions of stars and planets in our galaxy? Gravity! Did you know that Elisha defied gravity and caused an ax to float? Check it out in 2 Kings 6:1–7.

- What do people need in order to breathe on Earth? Oxygen.

- Has anyone tried to leave this world God created and explore outer space? Ever since 1961, when the Soviets launched *Vostok 1*, man has tried to fly into outer space to discover what else is out there. In 1969, Neil Armstrong became the first man to walk on the moon.

The U.S.S. Applepies

Veggie Fun!

Veggies in Space!

- What VeggieTales show takes place in outer space? *The Gourds Must Be Crazy* from *Are You My Neighbor?*

- Name the two VeggieTales characters who have the ability to fly. Snoodle Doo from *A Snoodle's Tale* and Hope from *An Easter Carol.*

- What was the name of the spaceship in *The Gourds Must Be Crazy*? The U.S.S. Applepies.

- In *Larry's Lagoon*, what was the professor's helicopter made of? Bamboo, Bamboo, Bamboo.

- In *Rack, Shack and Benny*, what unlikely flying machine did Laura Carrot pilot? A flying milk truck of course.

WEATHER

And God said, "Let there be lights in the expanse of the sky to separate the day from the night, and let them serve as signs to mark seasons and days and years, and let them be lights in the expanse of the sky to give light on the earth (Genesis 1:14).

Seasons

• What do we call the four seasons that God created? Summer, fall, winter, and spring.

• Did you know that the earth is divided into two hemispheres: the northern and southern? When one hemisphere experiences winter, the other enjoys summer! In most parts of the country, winter means colder temperatures and summer means warmer ones!

• What makes the seasons? God tilted the earth just a bit as it moves around the sun. The hemisphere that is tilted the closest enjoys a warmer climate. When the hemisphere tilts the other way, the sun is farther, and the climate turns cold.

• Have you heard the familiar saying, "Red sky at night, sailor's delight. Red sky in morning, sailors take warning"? This saying came from Matthew 16:1–3.

• When did the first rainbow appear? In the very first book of the Bible as a promise from God that he would never flood the entire earth again! (*Genesis 9:8–17*).

• Where in the Bible is the biggest flood? Genesis 6—9. It rained for forty days and nights, covered the mountains to a depth of more than twenty feet, killed everything that moved on the earth (except a man named Noah, his family, and the animals that were with them on the ark), and lasted for 150 days.

• What was the darkest day in history for Christians? The day Jesus was crucified. The sun did not shine for three hours, from noon until 3:00 pm. (*Luke 23:44–45*).

Extraordinary
Weather Sightings in the Bible . . .

- God has power over the wind and sea (*Job 28:22–27, Psalms 89:9; 107:29; Jonah 1; Matthew 14:22–33; Mark 4:35–41*).

- God enabled Moses to demonstrate his power through lightning and thunder (*Exodus 9:23; 10:13*).

- Although a "wind of hurricane force" wrecked Paul's ship while traveling on the Mediterranean Sea, he and all 276 people on board survived (*Acts 27:14*).

- Earthquakes sometimes symbolized God's judgment (*Numbers 16:31–33; Matthew 27:50–51; and Acts 16:26*).

- God made the sun and moon stand still for one day while Joshua was fighting the Amorites (*Joshua 1:1–14*).

- John saw hailstones coming down that weighed over one hundred pounds each (*Revelation 16:21*).

Stormy Weather

- Minnesota Cuke struggled through a blizzard in search of the Golden Carrot Nose from what giant snowman? The Indomitable Snowman of the North.

- The Pirates Who Don't Do Anything have never been to Boston in what season? The fall!

- Who saved the Vikings from the storm in *Lyle the Kindly Viking*? The Monks.

- In the Silly Song, "Love My Lips," what happened to Larry's lips when he was two? He left them out in the cold and they turned blue. What could he do?

GOD CREATED VEGETATION

Then God said, "Let the land produce vegetation: seed-bearing plants and trees on the land that bear fruit with seed in it, according to their various kinds" (Genesis 1:11).

Did you know that there are over 250,000 different kinds of plants in the world? And just think—God made them all!

- Where did the saying "the apple of your eye" come from? The Bible! *(Psalm 17:8).*

- What tree produces a popular oil used today? The olive tree *(Exodus 25:6).*

- How many times does wheat appear in the Bible? 46 times.

- What small seed did Jesus compare the kingdom of heaven to? A mustard seed *(Matthew 13:31).*

- What type of branches did people spread out for Jesus when he entered Jerusalem? Palm branches *(John 12:13).*

- What did the Lord provide Jonah so that he could have shade? A vine *(Jonah 4:6).*

- What is the tallest tree that God ever created? The Stratosphere Giant, a coast redwood, located in California. It's almost 370 feet tall!

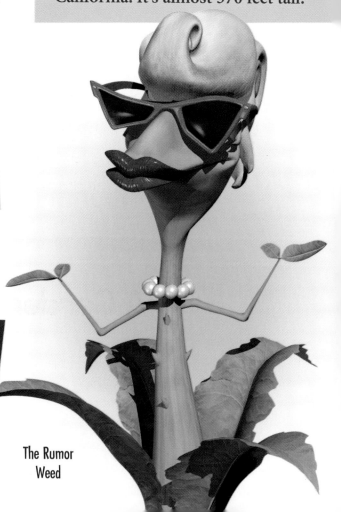

The Rumor
Weed

• Can you name the plants and trees that grew in the Bible times?

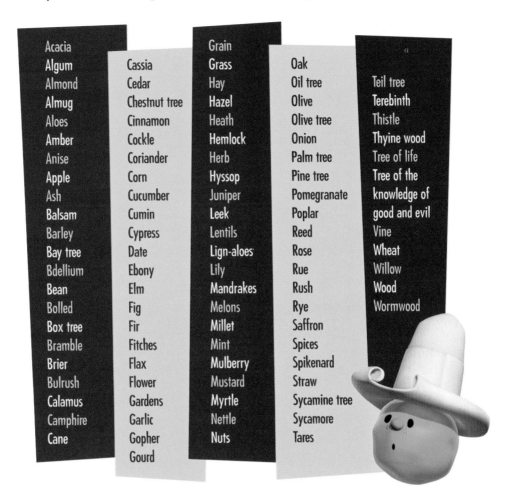

Acacia	Cassia	Grain	Oak	Teil tree
Algum	Cedar	Grass	Oil tree	Terebinth
Almond	Chestnut tree	Hay	Olive	Thistle
Almug	Cinnamon	Hazel	Olive tree	Thyine wood
Aloes	Cockle	Heath	Onion	Tree of life
Amber	Coriander	Hemlock	Palm tree	Tree of the
Anise	Corn	Herb	Pine tree	knowledge of
Apple	Cucumber	Hyssop	Pomegranate	good and evil
Ash	Cumin	Juniper	Poplar	Vine
Balsam	Cypress	Leek	Reed	Wheat
Barley	Date	Lentils	Rose	Willow
Bay tree	Ebony	Lign-aloes	Rue	Wood
Bdellium	Elm	Lily	Rush	Wormwood
Bean	Fig	Mandrakes	Rye	
Bolled	Fir	Melons	Saffron	
Box tree	Fitches	Millet	Spices	
Bramble	Flax	Mint	Spikenard	
Brier	Flower	Mulberry	Straw	
Bulrush	Gardens	Mustard	Sycamine tree	
Calamus	Garlic	Myrtle	Sycamore	
Camphire	Gopher	Nettle	Tares	
Cane	Gourd	Nuts		

A Garden Full of Veggies!

• What nasty plant sprouted rumors all over Bumblyburg? *The Rumor Weed.*

• How many different vegetables are named in the VeggieTales theme song? Eight: tomato, squash, potato, broccoli, celery, lima beans, collard greens, cauliflower.

GOD CREATED ANIMALS

- What is the definition for "creature"? A living being created by God.

First, God Created the Birds and the Fish

So God created the great creatures of the sea and every living and moving thing with which the water teems, according to their kinds, and every winged bird according to its kind (Genesis 1:21).

- Did you know that not all birds have the same kind of feathers and not all birds can fly?

- Can you name the different symbols that a dove stands for?
- Peace *(Genesis 8:8, 10)*
- Purity *(Song of Songs 5:2)*
- Affection *(Song of Songs 1:15; 2:14)*
- Holy Spirit *(Matthew 3:16; Mark 1:10; Luke 3:22; John 1:32)*
- Rest *(Psalm 55:6–8)*

- What is the bird that is first mentioned in the Bible? And the second? The raven *(Genesis 8:7)* and then the dove *(Genesis 8:8)*.

- What crested bird has a long bill and was considered unclean because it ate grub worms? Yuk! The hoopoe *(Leviticus 11:19)*.

- What is the first bird Noah sent out of the ark? A raven *(Genesis 8:7)*.

- What is the largest flightless bird in the Bible? The ostrich, which often grows to 108 inches tall and has a wingspan up to nearly fifteen feet across! *(Job 39:19)*.

- What large sea creature is described as having strong jaws, frightening teeth, and tough skin like a double armor? The leviathan—better to swim clear of that fellow! *(Job 41)*.

- What's the largest sea creature mentioned in the Bible that also swallowed a man and spit him out, completely unharmed, three days later? A big fish! Who was the man? Jonah *(Jonah 1:17)*.

- What symbol for Christians is based on the Greek word *ichthus* and stands for "Jesus Christ, Son of God, and Savior"? A fish.

Something Smells Fishy

- In what show did Larry's wind-up blue lobster first appear? *The Story of Flibber-o-loo.*

- In *Duke and the Great Pie War*, Duke has an interesting bird sculpted on top of his helmet. What type of bird is it? A chicken!

Scene from *The Toy That Saved Christmas*

- What kind of birds worked in Nezzer's Toy Factory in *The Toy That Saved Christmas*? The penguins.

- In *A Snoodle's Tale*, what kind of bird flies around Mount Ginchez? Red Snootered Finches.

- What bird is symbolized on King George's bathrobe? A ducky.

Then GOD CREATED the Rest of the ANIMALS

God said, "Let the land produce living creatures according to their kinds; livestock, creatures that move along the ground, and wild animals, each according to its kinds" (Genesis 1:24).

• What is the smallest animal mentioned in the Bible? The gnat! *(Exodus 8:16; Matthew 23:24).*

Interesting Animal Facts in the Bible:

• Other than humans, which mammals are most often mentioned in the Bible? If you guessed dogs—you are close. Dogs are mentioned 14 times. But the winner is . . . lions. Lions are named 130 times in the Bible!

• What king kept apes and baboons? Solomon *(1Kings 10:22).*

• What two animals talked in the Bible? A serpent *(Genesis 3:1–15)* and a donkey *(Numbers 22:28).*

• What's the best-dressed animal in the Bible? The camel, because they wore gold chains *(Judges 8:26).*

• What are five of the fastest animals in the Bible? The horse *(Exodus 14:9)*, falcon *(Isaiah 34:15)*, antelope and gazelle *(Deuteronomy 14:5)*, and the deer *(Isaiah 35:6).*

• Who was the lucky guy who got to name all the animals God created? Adam, the first man *(Genesis 2:19–20).*

Name Those Animals:

- What has soft, wet skin and can live on land or in water? Amphibians!

- What has dry, scaly skin and creates their own heat so that their body is the same temperature as their surroundings? Reptiles.

- What is warm-blooded and has hair or fur? Mammals! And yes . . . even whales and dolphins have just a bit of hair or fur!

- What mammals also live in the sea? Whale, dolphin and porpoise.

Striped or Small; Skinny or Tall— God Made Them All!

- Biggest mammal? The blue whale which can grow up to 115 feet long and weigh 130 tons!

- Tallest land mammal? The giraffe: Can grow to 18 feet high!

- Biggest bird? The ostrich: Can grow to 9 feet and weigh 345 pounds!

- Longest life? Clams and mollusks, which can live up to 376 years!

If You Like to Talk to the Animals ...

- In what Silly Song does Larry the Cucumber take care of the animals? "The Yodeling Veterinarian of the Alps!"

- What animals keep tipping over in *Dave and the Giant Pickle?* Sheep.

- According to Larry, what animal does everybody "got"? A water buffalo.

- Larry sings about an animal that's "kinda like a cow." What animal is it? A cebu.

- What kind of animal does Miss Achmetha sing about in *Esther: The Girl Who Became Queen*? Puppies.

GOD CREATED PEOPLE

So God created man in his own image, in the image of God he created him; male and female he created them (Genesis 1:27).

- What creature did God create after he was done making all the animals? Man.

- How is man different and more special than all the other creatures? Man was created in the image of God *(Genesis 1:27)*.

- What creature did God create from Adam's rib? A woman *(Genesis 2:21–22)*.

- Where did God place Adam and Eve? In the Garden of Eden.

- What was the actual date that God created Adam and Eve? Jewish people consider this date to be October 7, 3761 BC. This date is still used in calculating the year of the Jewish calendar today.

- Where is the Garden of Eden located? No one knows for certain. But you can read Genesis 2:1–14 for clues!

- Adam and Eve were the first people to disobey God in the Garden of Eden. What did they do? They disobeyed God when they ate from the tree of the knowledge of good and evil *(Genesis 3:6–7)*.

- What is the name of Adam and Eve's first baby? Cain *(Genesis 4:1)*. What was his brother's name? Abel *(Genesis 4:2)*.

VeggieTale Creations

- **What year were Bob and Larry created?**
1992.

- **How many different vegetables (and fruits) can you name that have been used in VeggieTales shows?** Here's a list to get you started.

Tomato
Gourd
Pea
Blueberry

Mushroom
Cucumber
Onion
Peach
Asparagus
Grape
Pear
Pickle
Pumpkin

Leek
Carrot
Scallion
Potato
Zucchini
Red Bell
    Pepper
Squash

Left to right:
Phillipe Pea, Pa Grape,
Larry the Cucumber, Apollo Gourd,
Bob the Tomato, Jimmy Gourd,
and Junior Asparagus

THE HUMAN BODY

I praise you because I am fearfully and wonderfully made (Psalm 139:14).

Facts and Figures about God's Creation of the Body

- **How many bones are you born with?** Babies are born with 300 bones, but as they grow into adults, their bones grow together, leaving them with only 206.

- **What part of your body has the thinnest skin?** The eyelid. The thickest skin? The sole of a foot.

- **The average person has how many hairs on their head?** Over 100,000!

- **How many nerve cells does the brain contain?** 100 billion, and each one can store about ten thousand bits of information!

- **What is the strongest muscle in the body?** The heart, and it's no bigger than the size of your fist.

- **What organ in the body cleans the blood?** The liver. What organ in the body holds food? The stomach.

- **What digests and breaks down food for the body to use?** The intestines.

- **How long would your small intestine be if it were all stretched out?** Up to thirty feet long!

- **What is the top layer of skin called?** The epidermis.

- **What sends signals and instructions to all parts of the body?** The brain.

- **What part of the bone is made up of flexible material?** Cartilage.

- **How do muscles work?** By getting shorter! They contract, pulling on the bones they are joined to, as they move.

- **How much saliva does a grown-up produce every day?** More than one liter!

- How long does it take for food to journey through the body? Between eighteen and forty-eight hours.

- What are the little sensitive spots on your tongue called? Taste buds.

- What are the five senses God created? Hearing, seeing, smelling, tasting and touching.

- How many words can the throat carry every day? About 18,000, enough to fill a 66-page book!

- Where is the smallest bone in your body located? Behind the eardrum.

- How many different sounds can the average adult ear recognize? About 330,000!

Look! No Hands!

- The creators of VeggieTales considered another type of food product before they decided on vegetables. What was it? Candy bars. But they decided that parents would appreciate vegetables more than sugary snacks.

- In *Sumo of the Opera*, what body part does Apollo Gourd use to defeat his opponents? His belly.

- In the Boyz in the Sink's debut song, what body part is Mr. Lunt missing? His belly button.

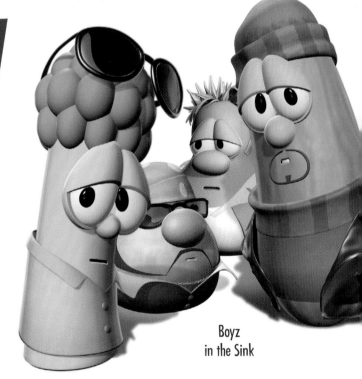

Boyz
in the Sink

- In the *Hairbrush Song*, which Veggie character is the only one who needs the hairbrush? The Peach, 'cause he's got hair.

AND THEN GOD RESTED

By the seventh day God had finished the work he had been doing; so on the seventh day he rested from all his work. And God blessed the seventh day and made it holy, because on it he rested from all the work of creating that he had done (Genesis 2:2–3).

Do you know that we're supposed to rest on the seventh day of the week? It's called the Sabbath, and God made it holy. On the seventh day of each week (Sunday, for most Christians), we should set time aside for worship, praise, and prayer to God. And don't forget to rest! That's important too!

• When was God most specific in commanding that people keep the Sabbath day as holy? In the fourth of the Ten Commandments: Exodus 20:8-11.

• God said there are six working days in Ezekiel 46:1. The Sabbath is not one of them.

• How many times is the Sabbath mentioned in the New Testament? Fifty-nine to sixty times (dependant upon the Bible translation).

• Jesus carefully taught how the Sabbath day should be observed (*Matthew 12:1–13*).

• Did God offer the Israelites a reward for keeping the Sabbath day holy? Yes, see Isaiah 58:13–14.

• God forbad the Israelites to work on the Sabbath, even during the busiest of times! (*Exodus 34:21*).

• Were people punished by God for breaking the Sabbath day? Yes, see Jeremiah 17:27.

Junior's bedroom isn't so scary . . . with the lights on!

Veggie Rest

- In *Where's God When I'm S-Scared*, why can't Junior go to sleep? Because he's scared.

- In *Asparagus of La Mancha*, what causes Don Quixote to have bad dreams? He eats too much hot salsa before he goes to bed.

- In *Daniel and the Lion's Den*, who has a dream and asks Daniel to interpret it? King Darius.

WHO IS GOD?

So God created man in his own image, in the image of God he created him; male and female he created them (Genesis 1:27).

God as Creator

Did you know . . .

that God created *you* in his image? That's pretty amazing. Of course, you don't really look just like God because God is a spirit. But you are a likeness of God in many ways!

Then God said, "Let us make man in our image, in our likeness, and let them rule over the fish of the sea and the birds of the air, over the livestock, over all the earth, and over all the creatures that move along the ground" (Genesis 1:26).

Can you name some of the ways we are made in God's likeness? Here are just some . . .

- God gave us the ability to know between right and wrong *(James 4:17).*

- **God made us with the ability to love.** Just like God has a deep love for us, we can feel and show love for others *(1 John 3:16).*

- **God made us with the ability to appreciate beauty.** We can look at what God made and know that it's beautiful! *(Genesis 2:9).*

- **God made us with the ability to forgive.** Just like he is merciful and forgiving *(Daniel 9:9),* God gave us the ability to forgive others *(Matthew 6:14).* When we do that, God promises to forgive us in return.

God at Work in the World ...

Through Creation!

- Did you know that Earth is the only planet in the solar system that can sustain life? God intended it that way when he shaped the earth as a home for us, because we are important to him! *(Psalms 24:1–2; 104:5–15).*

Through Miracles!

- Did you know that there are over one hundred miracles in the Old and New Testament combined? In fact, the Bible itself is a miracle, as it is the inspired Word of God *(2 Timothy 3:16).*

Through the Bible!

- God is all-powerful and whatever God says will happen *(Genesis 1:3).*
- God's Word is alive and given to us in the written word of the Bible. God's Word is true and when we read and follow it, things will change!
  God's Word is alive (*1 Peter 1: 23–25; Hebrews 4:12*).
  God's Word is eternal (lasts forever) (*Psalm 119:89*).
  God's Word is powerful (*Hebrews 4:12*).
  God's Word is truth (*John 17:17*).
  When we follow the truth, things change (*John 8:31–32*).

VeGGie Fun!

Where's God When I'm S-Scared?

In the VeggieTales show, *Where's God When I'm S-Scared?* Bob and Larry assure a frightened Junior that God is always in control!

- **What did Bob and Larry tell Junior that God was bigger than?** The boogie man, Godzilla, and the monsters on TV!

- **What do Bob and Larry say about God at the end of every show?** God made you special and he loves you very much!

GOD'S PROMISES

The Lord is not slow in keeping his promise, as some understand slowness. He is patient with you, not wanting anyone to perish, but everyone to come to repentance (2 Peter 3:9).

How many promises can you name?

Our God is an awesome God! He has made us lots and lots of promises to help us get through life.

- A promise of understanding *(Psalm 119:104)*.
- A promise of love *(Proverbs 8:17; John 3:16; 14:21)*.
- A promise of joy *(Isaiah 35:10)*.
- A promise to guide us *(Isaiah 42:16)*.
- A promise of forgiveness *(Colossians 3:13; Hebrews 8:12; 1 John 1:9)*.
- A promise of comfort when we're sad *(Isaiah 51:3)*.
- A promise of a wonderful life *(John 10:10)*.
- The promise of a home in heaven *(John 14:1–3)*.
- The promise of peace *(Psalm 85:8; John 14:27)*.
- The promise of resurrection *(Romans 8:11)*.
- The promise of gifts of the Spirit *(1 Corinthians 12)*.

- The promise to help us to grow through Christ *(Ephesians 4:11–15)*.
- The promise of strength *(Philippians 4:13)*.
- The promise of hope for the future *(Romans 5:5; Hebrews 6:19; 2 Timothy 1:12)*.
- The promise of rescue and freedom *(2 Timothy 4:18)*.
- The promise of rest *(Hebrews 4:9, 11)*.
- The promise to supply our needs *(John 15:7; Philippians 4:19)*.
- The promise of trust and faith *(John 14:1; Hebrews 6:18–19)*.
- The promise of wisdom *(James 1:5)*.
- The promise to care for us *(1 Peter 5:6–7)*.
- The promise of victory over death *(1 Corinthians 15:54–55; 1 John 5:4)*.
- The promise of answer to our prayers *(1 John 5:14)*.
- The promise of everlasting life *(Psalm 23:6; John 3:16; 4:13–14; 6:47)*.

How many promises were given in the Bible?

1,260! (NIV)

- Who are some Bible people that God made some big promises to?

Noah (*Genesis 6:18; 9:11*).
Abram (*Genesis 12:2–3, 7*).
Moses and the Israelites
    (*Deuteronomy 28:1–14*).
David (*2 Samuel 7:16*).
Israel (*Jeremiah 31:31–34*).

VeGGie Fun!

Larry's Promise

- In *Josh and the Big Wall*, what has God promised to Josh and the Israelites? They will enter the Promised Land (and it will be so grand.)

- In the song "Stand," Rack, Shack and Benny sing a song about standing up for what you believe in. In the song, what does God promise to do? He'll stand with you.

THE HOLY SPIRIT

The Holy Spirit is God's invisible but powerful presence.

Here are just some of the ways the Holy Spirit can help us!

- How can the Holy Spirit help you when you have a tough decision to make? He can help you distinguish between right and wrong *(John 16:7–8; Acts 4:19).*

- Who can help you when you're feeling lost and don't know which way to go? The Holy Spirit will guide you *(Psalm 48:14; John 16:13).*

- What do you do when you're worried about your problems? The Holy Spirit helps you make daily decisions *(Psalm 143:10).*

- When you feel like you're all alone, how can the Holy Spirit help? He is always present *(Psalm 139:7–8).*

- What if you're searching for answers? The Holy Spirit provides you with wisdom *(Isaiah 11:2).*

- What do you do when you're feeling tired? The Holy Spirit will give you rest *(Matthew 11:28).*

- How do you know how to act in a certain situation? The Holy Spirit will help you know what to do *(Ezekiel 36:26–27).*

- How can the Holy Spirit make you feel better? He is called "the Comforter" *(John 16:7* KJV*).*

- What if you need some cheering or support? The Holy Spirit is an encourager *(Acts 9:31).*

- What do you do when you're so upset you can't even pray? The Holy Spirit prays for us when we can't *(Romans 8:26).*

- What if you don't understand? The Holy Spirit is our internal teacher *(John 14:16–17, 26).*

- The Holy Spirit has many names just like God and Christ do. Can you name them? He is known as:

the Spirit of God *(Genesis 1:2)*,
the Spirit of the Lord *(Isaiah 61:1)*,
the Spirit of Christ *(Romans 8:9)*,
the Spirit of truth *(John 16:13)*,
the Spirit of grace *(Hebrews 10:29)*,
and the Comforter *(John 14:16* KJV).

- The Holy Spirit is a powerful gift. God encourages us to use that gift together as a people of God! When we do, we can come together as one body. Here's how that works:

Power of One

- **One Body** This is all the believers in the church.
- **One Spirit** The Holy Spirit works in us.
- **One Hope** Together, we all look toward heaven.
- **One Lord** Jesus Christ is our Lord.
- **One Faith** This is our one and only commitment to God.
- **One Baptism** This is our pledge of entry into God's family.
- **One God** God is our Father who watches over and loves us for all eternity.

VeGGie Fun!

What to do?

- In *Esther: The Girl Who Became Queen*, Mordecai challenges Esther to never be afraid to do what? To do what's right.

- In *Junior and the Bully*, Junior's dad tells him that God doesn't give us a spirit of fear but a spirit of what? A spirit of courage.

- What two VeggieTales characters helped Madame Blueberry see that God wants us to have a spirit of thankfulness? Junior and Annie.

THE NAMES & ATTRIBUTES OF GOD

In the Bible, names not only identified someone but told about the character of that person as well. How many of them can you name?

Lord *(Isaiah 42:8)*	Most High *(Psalm 47:2)*	Judge *(Genesis 18:25)*
Almighty *(Isaiah 6:3)*	Eternal *(Genesis 21:33)*	Peace *(Judges 6:24)*
All-Powerful *(Psalm 46:7)*	Holy One *(Isaiah 1:4)*	Creator *(Genesis 14:19)*
I AM *(Exodus 3:14)*	Father *(John 10:15)*	

What Is God's Personality Like?

- What can you read to find out God's personality? Read the Bible. It has many verses that tell of God's personality and attributes *(Psalm 145:3, 5–6)*.

- Has your mom or dad ever said they have "eyes in the back of their heads" and are watching you? That's sort of silly, but God really does see everything, and he knows everything too. That's why he is called *omniscient (Job 37:16)*.

- What does the word *omni* mean? It means "all."

- Did you know that "God is eternal" means that he has no beginning and no end? *(Psalm 102:24–27)*.

- Have you ever been somewhere and wished that someone could help you through those scared and lonely feelings? God can be with you all the time, no matter where you are. That's called *omnipresent (Job 37:16)*.

- Who do you think of when you think of a powerful superhero? Batman, Superman, Spiderman? Well, God is more powerful than any superhero you can imagine. He is *omnipotent*, meaning that he is "all powerful" *(Matthew 19:26)*.

How well do you know God?

How many of his attributes can you name?

GOD . . .

- is eternal
  (Psalm 102:24–27)
- is faithful
  (Deuteronomy 32:4)
- is omnipotent
  (Matthew 19:26)
- is omnipresent
  (Psalm 46:1)
- is omniscient
  (Psalm 139:1–4)
- is holy
  (Revelation 15:4)
- is our redeemer
  (Psalm 19:14)

- is merciful
  (Titus 3:4–5)
- is truth *(Psalm 31:5)*
- is majestic
  (Psalm 8:1)
- is perfect
  (Matthew 5:48)
- is love
  (1 John 4:16)
- is changeless
  (James 1:17)
- is jealous
  (Exodus 20:5)

- made all things
  (Psalm 24:1–2)
- is a provider
  (Psalm 65:9)
- is righteous
  (Psalm 4:1)
- is forgiving
  (1 John 1:9)
- is spirit *(John 4:24)*
- is our rock
  and refuge
  (2 Samuel 22:3)
- is fair
  (Acts 10:34–35)
- is supreme
  (Revelation 15:4)

- is a healer
  (Exodus 15:26)
- is patient
  (2 Peter 3:9)
- is gracious
  (Psalm 145:8)
- is great
  (Psalm 145:3)
- is our shepherd
  (Psalm 23:1)
- is wise
  (Romans 16:27)
- speaks to us
  through his Son
  (Hebrews 1:1–3)

Know Your Veggies

What VeggieTales character best fits the descriptions below:
- He's round, red, and particular. Bob the Tomato.
- He's well-intentioned but always silly. Larry the Cucumber.
- He's tall, green, and grammatically precise. Archibald Asparagus.
- He's a pleasant yellow fellow and, with his brother's help, he can eat most anything! Jerry Gourd.
- He is that Hero! LarryBoy.

GOD'S COMMANDS

As God, our Father, he leads and guides us by giving us rules to obey. How did we get those rules and what are they? Take a look . . .

- What is the name of God's special rules for daily living called? The Ten Commandments *(Deuteronomy 4:13).*

- Who received those rules from God? Moses *(Exodus 31:18).*

- Where can you find those rules in the Bible? Exodus 20:1–17.

What Are the Ten Commandments?

1. "I am the LORD your God, who brought you out of Egypt, out of the land of slavery. You shall have no other gods before me" *(Exodus 20:2–3).*

2. "You shall not make for yourself an idol in the form of anything in heaven above or on the earth beneath or in the waters below. You shall not bow down to them or worship them" *(Exodus 20:4–5).*

3. "You shall not misuse the name of the LORD your God, for the LORD will not hold anyone guiltless who misuses his name" *(Exodus 20:7).*

4. "Remember the Sabbath day by keeping it holy" *(Exodus 20:8).*

5. "Honor your father and your mother" *(Exodus 20:12).*

6. "You shall not murder" *(Exodus 20:13).*

7. "You shall not commit adultery" *(Exodus 20:14).*

8. "You shall not steal" *(Exodus 20:15).*

9. "You shall not give false testimony against your neighbor" *(Exodus 20:16).*

10. "You shall not covet your neighbor's house. You shall not covet your neighbor's wife, or his manservant or maidservant, his ox or donkey, or anything that belongs to your neighbor" *(Exodus 20:17).*

When God was giving Moses the Ten Commandments, the people became impatient and built an idol to worship. What was their punishment? Moses burned the calf they had created as an idol in the fire and ground it up into dust. Then he put the gold dust in the Israelites' water and made them drink it *(Exodus 32:19–20)*.

God gave Moses 613 commands! They are recorded in Exodus 20:1—Numbers 10:10.

Jesus summed up all the commands in just two. Matthew 22:37–39 says: *"Jesus replied: 'Love the Lord your God with all your heart and with all your soul and with all your mind.' This is the first and greatest commandment. And the second is like it: 'Love your neighbor as yourself.'"*

• How many commands did God provide in the New Testament? 1,051.

Moses and More

• In the VeggieTales story *Babysitter in DeNile,* who played the title role of the babysitter in DeNile? Laura Carrot played Moses's sister, Miriam.

PRAYER

Do not be anxious about anything, but in everything, by prayer and petition, with thanksgiving, present your requests to God (Philippians 4:6).

God Loves for His People to Pray to Him

Daniel lived in a country where there were only a few people who believed in God. There was even a rule that people could not pray to anyone except the king! When the king found out that Daniel prayed to God, he had Daniel put in a den of hungry lions.

- What did God do when Daniel prayed to him from the lions' den? God shut the lions' mouths so they couldn't eat Daniel! *(Daniel 6:21–22).*

Elijah was a prophet of God. There were also prophets of the idol Baal. There was a contest to see who was greater—God or Baal. The prophets built altars and had a sacrifice on the altar. The prophets of Baal called on their god to send fire from heaven to burn up the sacrifice. Nothing happened. Before Elijah prayed to God, he poured water on the altar.

- What did God do when Elijah prayed to him? God sent so much fire from heaven, it burned up the sacrifice, the water, the wood, even the stones and the soil *(1 Kings 18:38).*

Types of Prayers

- **Mealtime prayers:** To thank God for your food.

- **Bedtime prayers:** Talk to God about your day to say thank you for all the blessings he gave you today!

When to ⬬pray⬭ and what to say:

- When you need to admit that you have done something wrong: Tell God that you are sorry *(Psalm 51; 1 John 1:9)*.

- When you need to tell God you are sorry for doing something wrong: Ask God to forgive you *(Daniel 9:4–19; Luke 11:4)*.

- When you are feeling joy, worship, or you wish to show honor and respect to God: Praise God to tell him how wonderful He is *(1 Chronicles 29:10–13; Luke 1:46–55)*.

- When you are feeling grateful: Pray a prayer of thanksgiving *(Psalm 105:1–7; 1 Thessalonians 5:16–18)*.

- When you want to ask God for something: Just ask God; he loves to give good gifts to his children *(Genesis 24:12–14; Matthew 7:11)*.

- When you need to ask God for help on behalf of someone else: Intercession means asking God to help that person *(Exodus 32:11–13; Philippians 1:9–11)*.

- When you want to tell God that you trust him: Offer a prayer of faith *(Psalm 23; Luke 2:29–32)*.

Larry the Cucumber as Little Joe

VeGGie Fun!

Prayer Time

- In the show *The Ballad of Little Joe*, where is Little Joe when he prays to God and asks, "What's going on here?" In jail.

- In the show *Madame Blueberry*, who sings a song of thankfulness that touches Madame Blueberry's heart? Annie.

37

ANSWERS TO PRAYER

This is the confidence we have in approaching God: that if we ask anything according to his will, he hears us. And if we know that he hears us—whatever we ask—we know that we have what we asked of him (1 John 5:14–15).

How do you know that God listens to and hears your prayers?

The Bible tells us that God and Jesus listen and hear our prayers!

• **Who asked Jesus how to pray?** His disciples. Jesus gave them an explanation by teaching them what we now call the Lord's Prayer *(Matthew 6:9–13; Luke 11:2–4).*

Prayer requires faith and when you have faith in God, Jesus explained that your prayers will be answered. What do you have to do for that to happen? Ask!

So I say to you: Ask and it will be given to you; seek and you will find; knock and the door will be opened to you. For everyone who asks receives; he who seeks finds; and to him who knocks, the door will be opened (Luke 11:9–10).

There's an easy way to remember what Jesus wants us to know when we pray. Simply use the word . . .

• **Adoration** or praise of God *(Isaiah 42:12)*
• **Confess** our sins *(1 John 1:9)*
• **Thank** God for things he has given us *(Philippians 4:6)*
• **Supplication**—asking for God's help for ourselves and others *(James 5:16)*

• **Do you know what *adoration* means?** It means to tell someone how wonderful they are and how good they are at doing things. David prayed many prayers of adoration in the Book of Psalms (see Psalm 19).

Veggie Fun!

Jonah-a VeggieTales Movie

- In *Jonah—a VeggieTales Movie,* Jonah prays to God and receives instructions to go to what fish-slapping city? Nineveh.

- Did Jonah obey God's directions and go to Nineveh? No, he went the other direction.

- Jonah prays again when he's on top of the hill looking down on Nineveh. What does he ask God to do? To destroy Nineveh.

EXTRAORDINARY PRAYER STORIES

The Bible is filled with . . .
extraordinary people who provide us with wonderful
models of prayer and how God responded to them:

- Abraham's prayer in Genesis 15:2–3.
- Isaac's prayer in Genesis 25:21–23.
- Moses's prayer in Exodus 9:29.
- Moses and Miriam's prayer in Exodus 15.

- Joshua's prayer in Joshua 10:12–13.
- Gideon's prayer in Judges 6:36–40.
- Samson's prayer in Judges 16:28–31.

- David's prayer in 2 Samuel 7:18–29.
- Hannah's prayers in 1 Samuel 1:9–11; 2:1–10.
- Elisha's prayer in 2 Kings 4:33–35.
- Hezekiah's prayer in 2 Kings 19:14–19.
- Solomon's prayer in 1 Kings 3:5–9; 8:23–53.

- Ezra's prayers in Ezra 8:21–23.
- Job's prayers in Job 3:3–12; 10:18–22.
- Elijah's prayers in 1 Kings 17:20–21; 18:36–37.

- David's prayers in the Book of Psalms.
- Daniel's prayers in Daniel 6:10–23; 9:3–19.

- The priest's and the Levite's prayers in 2 Chronicles 30:25–27.
- Jonah's prayers in Jonah 2; 4:1–11.

- Mary's prayer in Luke 1:46–55.
- Simeon and Anna's prayer in Luke 2:28–38.
- Stephen's prayer in Acts 7:59–60.
- Peter's prayer in Acts 9:36–43.
- Jesus's prayer in John 17.

- Mary, the women, and the people's prayer in Acts 1:14.
- Peter, John, and the people's prayer in Acts 4:24–25.

- The people's prayer in Acts 12:5.
- The church's prayer in Acts 13:3.

- Paul and Barnabas's prayer in Acts 14:23.
- Paul's prayer in Romans 10:1; Philippians 1:9–11.
- Epaphras's prayer in Colossians 4:12.

Ever wonder when you really should pray? All the time! (*1 Thessalonians 5:17*).

Time to Pray!

- In the VeggieTales story *Daniel and the Lions' Den*, Daniel knows that God's law says you should pray only to whom? Only to God.

- In that same story, just before the wise men burst in, Daniel is praying. What does he pray about? He thanks God for the sunshine, for all his friends, and for the courage to do what's right, even when he knows it could get him in trouble.

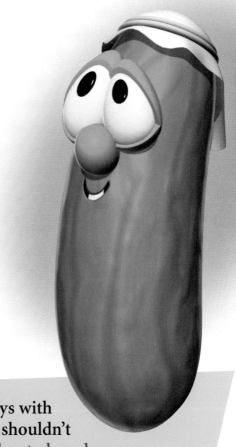

- In *An Easter Carol*, after the pastor prays with Edmund, he reminds Edmund that he shouldn't worry, and he has to have "what"? He has to have hope, that no matter what happens, God is taking care of us.

WHO IS JESUS?

And a voice from heaven said, "This is my Son, whom I love; with him I am well pleased" (Matthew 3:17).

Jesus was the long-awaited king whom God promised he would send to his people! Jesus is God's Son, who came to earth to teach, to love, and to forgive our sins and offer us life everlasting through his death and resurrection!

The name *Jesus* means Christ—anointed one; Yeshua—salvation; and Immanuel—God with us. Here are some others:

Jesus:

- Son of God
  (Mark 1:1)
- Son of Man
  (Matthew 8:20)
- Mighty God
  (Isaiah 9:6)
- Prince of Peace
  (Isaiah 9:6)
- Son of David
  (Matthew 15:22)
- Lamb of God
  (John 1:29)
- Rabbi/Teacher
  (John 1:38)
- Alpha and Omega
  (Revelation 1:8)

- King of Kings
  (Revelation 19:16)
- Lord of Lords
  (Revelation 19:16)
- Prince of Peace
  (Isaiah 9:6)
- Messiah
  (Matthew 1:1)
- Good Shepherd
  (John 10:11)
- Way, Truth & Life
  (John 14:6)
- Author of Life
  (Acts 3:15)

- Bread of Life
  (John 6:35)
- Deliverer
  (Romans 11:26)
- Resurrection & Life
  (John 11:25)
- Rock
  (1 Corinthians 10:4)
- Vine
  (John 15:1)
- Wonderful Counselor
  (Isaiah 9:6)
- Everlasting Father
  (Isaiah 9:6)
- Light of the World
  (John 8:12)

Prophecy Fulfilled

- What does the word *prophecy* mean? It means "forth telling," which means the telling of the future.

Much of Jesus's ministry was foretold in the Old Testament. Do you know where?

- Micah 5:2 said that Jesus would be born in Bethlehem. It was fulfilled in Matthew 2:1.

- Psalm 41:9 foretold that one of Jesus's followers would betray him.

It was fulfilled in Matthew 26:14–16, 47–50; Mark 14:10.

- Zechariah 9:9 said that Jesus would ride into Jerusalem on a donkey. It was fulfilled in Matthew 21:1–5.

- Isaiah 53:7–9 said Jesus would be tried and condemned. It was fulfilled in Luke 23:1–25; Matthew 27:1–2.

- Isaiah 53:4–5 said that Jesus would take our pain and bear our suffering as we punished him. It was fulfilled in Matthew 8:16–17.

- Psalm 22:6–8 foretold that Jesus would be made fun of and insulted. It was fulfilled in Matthew 27:39–44; Luke 23:11, 35–39.

- Isaiah 53:12 said that Jesus would be crucified and pray for his enemies. It was fulfilled in Matthew 27:38; Mark 15:27–28; Luke 23:32–34.

- Psalm 16:10 said that Jesus would be raised from the dead. It was fulfilled in Matthew 28:1–10; Luke 24:1–5; Acts 2:22–32.

Buzz-Saw Louie to the Rescue!

- What was the very first VeggieTales Christmas show? *The Toy That Saved Christmas.*

- Mr. Nezzer made Buzz-Saw Louie toys for all the boys and girls of Dinkletown. What message did Buzz-Saw Louie deliver to the kids? "You need more toys!"

- One very special Buzz-Saw Louie toy comes to the rescue to help do what? Help everyone discover the real meaning of Christmas—Jesus!

JESUS IS BORN!

Suddenly a great company of the heavenly host appeared with the angel, praising God and saying, "Glory to God in the highest, and on earth peace to men on whom his favor rests" (Luke 2:13–14).

• **What did the angel tell Joseph?** Not to be afraid to take Mary home as his wife *(Matthew 1:20).*

• **Who told people to get ready for the birth of Jesus?** John the Baptist. *I baptize you with water for repentance. But after me will come one who is more powerful than I, whose sandals I am not fit to carry. He will baptize you with the Holy Spirit and with fire (Matthew 3:11).*

• **Why did Mary and Joseph go to Bethlehem?** To register for a census. *In those days Caesar Augustus issued a decree that a census should be taken of the entire Roman world. (This was the first census that took place while Quirinius was governor of Syria.) And everyone went to his own town to register (Luke 2:1–3).*

• **Who told Mary that she would be the mother of Jesus?** An angel named Gabriel. *In the sixth month, God sent the angel Gabriel to Nazareth, a town in Galilee, to a virgin pledged to be married to a man named Joseph, a descendant of David. The virgin's name was Mary . . . But the angel said to her, "Do not be afraid, Mary, you have found favor with God. You will be with child and give birth to a son, and you are to give him the name Jesus" (Luke 1:26–27, 30–31).*

• **Who appeared in the sky?** Angels. *Suddenly a great company of the heavenly host appeared with the angel, praising God and saying, "Glory to God in the highest, and on earth peace to men on whom his favor rests" (Luke 2:13-14).*

• **Who told the shepherds about Jesus's birth?** An angel. *An angel of the Lord appeared to them, and the glory of the Lord shone around them, and they were terrified. But the angel said to them, "Do not be* *afraid. I bring you good news of great joy that will be for all the people. Today in the town of David a Savior has been born to you; he is Christ the Lord. This will be a sign to you: You will find a baby wrapped in cloths and lying in a manger" (Luke 2:9–12).*

- Why was Jesus born in a stable? There was no room in the inn.

- Where did Mary put the new baby Jesus? A manger. *While they were there, the time came for the*

baby to be born, and she gave birth to her firstborn, a son. She wrapped him in cloths and placed him in a manger, because there was no room for them in the inn (Luke 2:6–7).

- What did the wise men present to Jesus upon their visit? Gold, frankincense, and myrrh. *On coming to the house, they saw the child with his mother Mary, and they bowed down and worshiped him. Then they opened their treasures and presented him with gifts of gold and of incense and of myrrh (Matthew 2:11).*

The Star of Christmas

Pa Grape as Seymour in *The Star of Christmas*

- In *The Star of Christmas*, what church hosts the real Christmas pageant? Saint Barts.

- In the Christmas pageant, what Veggie characters play the sheep? The peas, dressed in lots of cotton balls.

- Cavis and Millward are in search of a famous actress to be in their play. Who is she, and what Veggie character plays that role? Miss Effie Pickering was played by Madame Blueberry.

- What is the lesson that Cavis and Millward want all the people of London to learn? How to love.

CELEBRATING JESUS'S BIRTH

Every year, people all over the world celebrate the birth of Jesus on December 25. We call that celebration Christmas!

Christmas and Its Traditions

• **What does the word *Christmas* mean?** "Mass of Christ," which was later shortened to Christmas.

• **Where did the word *Xmas* originate?** It was first used in Europe in the 1500s. It comes from the Greek alphabet, in which *X* is the very first letter of Christ's name: *Xristos.*

• **Who were the wise men in the Bible?** They were magi—scholars who specialized in astrology, medicine, and natural science.

• **When did the magi visit the Christ child?** Many Bible scholars think that the visit of the magi was two years after Jesus's birth! *(Matthew 2:16).*

• **Why do we deck the halls with boughs of holly?** The berries symbolize the blood of Jesus, and the thorny leaves represent his crown of thorns.

• **Why do people hang up Christmas lights?** Some say the tradition of stringing lights at Christmas honors the early Christians, who were persecuted for what they believed. To signal that church was being held in someone's home, a single candle was lit in that window.

• **Why are poinsettias the official plant of Christmas?** They were brought to the United States from Mexico in 1828 by Dr. Joel Poinsett. The Mexicans believed the plant resembled the Star of Bethlehem.

- **What do candy canes have to do with Christmas?** Choir masters would give this "staff" shaped candy to represent Christ as the Good Shepherd.

- **What does the name *Bethlehem* mean?** In Hebrew, it means "house of bread." Jesus is the bread of life (*John 6:35*).

Larry, Bob, and the Peach in a Scene from "Oh, Santa"

VeggieTales Christmas Music

- **On the VeggieTales Christmas album *The Incredible Singing Christmas Tree*, what do Mr. Nezzer and Mr. Lunt say is the sound of Christmas time?** Jingle, Jingle, Jingle ka-Ching.

- **Who wondered "If the baby Jesus bounced on his Daddy's knee" in the song "Was He a Boy Like Me?"** Junior Asparagus.

- **In the Silly Song "Oh Santa," who comes to visit Larry the Cucumber?** A robber, a viking, an agent of the IRS and Santa.

- **What does Larry offer three of these visitors?** A yummy cookie.

JESUS'S MINISTRY

- **When did Jesus begin his ministry?** With his baptism by John the Baptist *(Matthew 3:13–17)*.

- **What was the first significant event in Jesus's ministry?** His temptation by Satan *(Matthew 4:1–11)*.

- **To whom did Jesus tell that you must be born again?** To a man named Nicodemus *(John 3:16-17)*.

How long was Jesus's ministry?

He began his ministry when he was about thirty years of age *(Luke 3:23)*.

Jesus's first recorded Passover observance was recorded in John 2:13, about six months after his ministry began in the fall of the previous year.

Jesus celebrated three other Passovers recorded in John 5:1; John 6:4; and the last one, with his disciples recorded in John 11:55.

Because the Passovers were an annual event, the total of his ministry would be three and one half years!

- Jesus traveled to many different places throughout his ministry. Can you name some of them?

Bethlehem — *(Matthew 2:1)*

Nazareth — *(Matthew 2:23)*

Bethany — *(Matthew 21:17; 26:6; Mark 11:1; 14:3; Luke 19:29; 24:50; John 11:1; 12:1)*

Jericho — *(Matthew 20:29; Mark 10:46; Luke 18:35; 19:1)*

Jerusalem — *(Matthew 4:25; 16:21; 20:17; Mark 1:5; 10:32; 11:11; Luke 18:31)*

Emmaus — *(Luke 24:13–29)*

Cana — *(John 2:1; 4:46)*

Capernaum — *(Matthew 4:13; 8:5; Mark 1:21; Luke 4:31)*

Bethsaida — *(Mark 6:45; 8:22)*

Caesarea Philippi — *(Matthew 16:13; Mark 8:27)*

Mount of Olives — *(Matthew 21:1; 24:3; Mark 11:1; Luke 21:37)*

Nain — *(Luke 7:11)*

Gerasenes — *(Mark 5:1; Luke 8:26)*

Plain of Gennesaret — *(Matthew 14:34; Mark 6:53)*

Decapolis — *(Mark 7:31)*

Tyre and Sidon — *(Matthew 15:21; Mark 7:24)*

Magadan/Dalmanutha — *(Matthew 15:39; Mark 8:10)*

Samaria — *(Luke 17:11; John 4:5)*

Judea — *(Matthew 19:1; Mark 10:1)*

Ephraim — *(John 11:54)*

- Jesus performed four different types of miracles. What were they?

Miracles of Nature—He stopped a storm on the sea and walked on water.

Miracles of Healing—He healed many from their illnesses.

Miracles over Evil Spirits—He commanded demons out.

Miracles over Death—He raised Lazarus and the daughter of Jairus from death. Most of all, Jesus himself arose from death!

See page 142, WONDERS, MIRACLES, & AMAZING STUFF for a list of Jesus's miracles.

Jesus Forgives 6

- Jesus specifically forgave six different people during his ministry on earth. Who were they?

The paralytic who was lowered on a mat through a roof *(Matthew 9:2–8)*.

The woman caught in adultery *(John 8:3–11)*.

The woman who anointed his feet with oil *(Luke 7:47–50)*.

Peter, for denying he knew Jesus *(John 18:15–18, 25–27; 21:15–19)*.

The criminal on the cross *(Luke 23:39–43)*.

The people who crucified him *(Luke 23:34)*.

VeGGie Fun!

Oh, Where Are My Veggies?

- What town is LarryBoy from? Bumblyburg.

- What town does Larry NOT want to go to in *The Toy That Saved Christmas*? Puggslyville, because the bridge is out.

- Where does the show *Duke and the Great Pie War* take place? The Kingdom of Scone.

- Name the five places on the map where Minnesota Cuke travels? Moose Lake, Lombard, Franklin, Malta, Seville.

- In the VeggieTales show *Are You My Neighbor?* what two towns did Larry the Cucumber get stuck between? Flibber-o-loo and Jibberty-lot.

JESUS TEACHES

Jesus taught us best by his own example in the way in which he lived his life. But Jesus also had many special teaching times too.

The Sermon on the Mount

This was a special sermon that Jesus gave to his disciples to teach what he wants from those who follow him. By living this way, Jesus said that we will be "blessed," which is a promise of joy we receive as a member of God's family.

Poor in Spirit	Thinking that others are as important as you are.	The reward is the kingdom of heaven.
Mourn	Believing in God even when life on earth is hard.	The reward is comfort.
Meekness	You don't have to be the boss.	The reward is to inherit the earth.
Righteousness	Always try to follow God's teaching.	The reward is to be filled.
Mercy	Willingness to show forgiveness to others.	The reward is being shown mercy.
Pure in heart	Being truthful and kind.	The reward is to see God.
Peacemaker	Not arguing or fighting.	The reward is to be called the sons of God.
Persecuted	People treat you badly because you are a Christian.	The reward is to inherit the kingdom of heaven.

Jesus Teaches and Helps Many

Who are the people Jesus taught or helped?

- Followers who fish for sea critters: Fishermen *(Matthew 4:18–20)*.
- Someone who gathers money for Rome: A tax collector *(Matthew 9:9)*.
- Someone who knows all the laws: An expert in law *(Matthew 22:35)*.
- Someone who was unable to walk: A paralyzed man *(Mark 2:1–12)*.
- A church leader: A synagogue ruler *(Mark 5:22)* and religious leader *(John 3:1–21)*.
- Someone in need of healing: A sick woman *(Mark 5:25–34)* and a person with leprosy *(Luke 17:11–19)*.
- Someone who cannot see: A blind man *(Mark 10:46–52)*.

- Little ones: A young boy *(Mark 9:17–27)* and children *(Mark 10:13–16)*.
- A wealthy person: A rich man *(Mark 10:17–23)*.
- A politician and a soldier: A Roman governor *(Mark 15:1–15)* and a Roman centurion *(Luke 7:1–10)*.
- A penniless woman without a husband: A poor widow *(Luke 7:11–17; 21:1–4)*.
- Someone who did something illegal: A criminal *(Luke 23:40–43)*.
- A disciple who did not believe: A doubting follower *(John 20:24–29)*.

What We Have Learned

Larry as the Italian Scallion

- In the VeggieTales show *Dave and the Giant Pickle*, Junior Asparagus learns that with God's help, little guys can do what? Big things too.

- In the show *Sumo of the Opera* what lesson does the Italian Scallion learn when he faces Apollo Gourd for the Sumo Championship? To persevere and finish what you start.

JESUS'S PARABLES

Jesus spoke all these things to the crowd in parables; he did not say anything to them without using a parable (Matthew 13:34).

God as Creator

When Jesus told parables to the people, it helped him to teach God's messages in new, interesting and meaningful ways.

Parables: Where to find it:

- Lamp under a basket . . . . *Matthew 5:14–16; Mark 4:21–22; Luke 8:16–17; 11:33–36*
- Wise and foolish builders . . . . *Matthew 7:24–27; Luke 6:47–49*
- Unshrunk (new) cloth on an old garment . . . . *Matthew 9:16; Mark 2:21; Luke 5:36*
- New wine in old wineskins . . . . *Matthew 9:17; Mark 2:22; Luke 5:37–38*
- The sower and the soils . . . . *Matthew 13:3–8, 18–23; Mark 4:3–8, 14–20; Luke 8:5–8, 11–15*
- The tares (weeds) . . . . *Matthew 13:24–30*
- The mustard seed . . . . *Matthew 13:31–32; Mark 4:30–32; Luke 13:18–19*
- The yeast in the dough . . . . *Matthew 13:33; Luke 13:20–21*
- The treasure and the pearl . . . . *Matthew 13:44–46*
- The fisherman's net . . . . *Matthew 13:47–50*
- The lost sheep . . . . *Matthew 18:12–14; Luke 15:4–7*
- The unforgiving servant . . . . *Matthew 18:23–34*
- The workers in the vineyard . . . . . . *Matthew 20:1–16*
- The two sons . . . . *Matthew 21:28–32*
- The wicked vinedressers . . . . *Matthew 21:33–44; Mark 12:1–11; Luke 20:9–18*
- The wedding banquet . . . . *Matthew 22:2–14*
- Leaves on the fig tree . . . . *Matthew 24:32–35; Mark 13:28–29; Luke 21:29–31*
- Ten young women . . . . *Matthew 25:1–13*
- Bags of gold . . . . *Matthew 25:14–30; Luke 19:11–27*

- The growing seed. . . . . *Mark 4:26–29*
- Return of the house owner . . . . . . *Mark 13:35–37*
- The creditor and two debtors . . . . *Luke 7:41–43*
- The good samaritan . . . . *Luke 10:30–37*
- The friend in need. . . . . *Luke 11:5–8*
- The rich fool . . . . *Luke 12:16–21*
- The watchful servants. . . . . *Luke 12:35–40*
- The barren fig tree . . . . *Luke 13:6–9*
- The great supper . . . . *Luke 14:16–24*
- Building a tower . . . . *Luke 14:28–33*
- The lost sheep . . . . *Luke 15:4–7*
- The lost coin . . . . *Luke 15:8–10*
- The lost son . . . . *Luke 15:11–32*
- The dishonest manager . . . . *Luke 16:1–8*
- The rich man and Lazarus . . . . *Luke 16:19–31*
- Servants and their duty . . . . *Luke 17:7–10*
- The unjust judge and
  persistent widow . . . . *Luke 18:2–8*
- The pharisee and the tax collector . . *Luke 18:10–14*
- The rich man's servants . . . . *Luke 19:12–27*

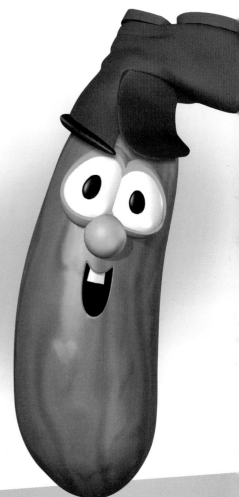

Love Your Neighbor!

- What show is a VeggieTales retelling of the parable "The Good Samaritan"? *The Story of Flibber-o-loo* from the show *Are You My Neighbor?*

- In *The Story of Flibber-o-loo*, Larry the Cucumber went for a walk outside the walls of Flibber-o-loo. Who did he take with him? His pet wind-up blue lobster.

- What happened to this Flibbian as he walked with his lobster? He was robbed by three scallions and left in a hole.

- Who rescued the Flibbian from the hole and took him back to the doctor in Flibber-o-loo? A little boy from Jibberty-lot played by Junior Asparagus.

JESUS'S LAST DAYS

What were the events during the last week of Jesus's life?

Jesus's Last Week

Sunday

- Jesus's triumphant entry into Jerusalem—*(Matthew 21:1–11; Mark 11:1–10; Luke 19:29–40; John 12:12–19).*

Monday

- Jesus cleared the temple *(Matthew 21:12–13; Mark 11:15–18; Luke 19:45–46; John 2:13–16).*

Tuesday

- The authority of Jesus questioned—*(Matthew 21:23–27; Mark 11:27–33; Luke 20:1–8).*
- Jesus teaches in the temple *(Matthew 21:28—23:39; Mark 12:1–44; Luke 20:9—21:4).*
- Jesus anointed—*(Matthew 26:6–13; Mark 14:3–9; John 12:2–11).*

Wednesday

- Plot against Jesus—*(Matthew 26:3–5).*
- Judas agrees to betray Jesus—*(Matthew 26:14–16; Mark 14:10–11; Luke 22:3–6).*

Thursday

- The Last Supper—*(Matthew 26:17–29; Mark 14:12–25; Luke 22:7–20).*

- Jesus prays in the Garden of Gethsemane—*(Matthew 26:36–46; Mark 14:32–42; Luke 22:39–46; John 18:1).*

- Jesus is betrayed by Judas and arrested—*(Matthew 26:47–56; Mark 14:43–52; Luke 22:47–53; John 18:2–11).*

Friday

• Jesus is on trial—
  (*Matthew 26:57—
  27:2, 11–31;
  Mark 14:53—15:20;
  Luke 22:54—23:25;
  John 18:12—19:16*).

• Peter denies Jesus—
  (*Matthew 26:58, 69–75;
  Mark 14:54, 66–72;
  Luke 22:54–62;
  John 18:15-18; 25–27*).

• Jesus is crucified—
  (*Matthew 27:32–56;
  Mark 15:21–41;
  Luke 23:26–49;
  John 19:17–30*).

Sunday

• Jesus is resurrected—
  (*Matthew 28:1–10;
  Mark 16:1–11;
  Luke 24:1–12;
  John 20:1–18*).

Oh, No, What Ya Gonna Do?

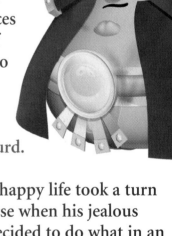

• In the Veggie show *Sumo of the Opera*, The Italian Scallion faces the fight of his life. Who does he meet in the ring? Apollo Gourd.

• Little Joe's happy life took a turn for the worse when his jealous brothers decided to do what in an effort to get rid of him? They threw him in the mineshaft.

• In the VeggieTales show *Esther: The Girl Who Became Queen*, what characters get banished to the Isle of Perpetual Tickling for trying to drop a piano on the king's head? The Peaoni brothers.

JESUS'S DEATH AND RESURRECTION

The last words spoken by Jesus on the cross reveal a great deal about who he was and what he did.

- *My God, my God, why have you forsaken me? (Matthew 27:46; Mark 15:34).*

- *Father, forgive them, for they do not know what they are doing (Luke 23:34).*

- *I tell you the truth, today you will be with me in paradise (Luke 23:43).*

- *Father, into your hands I commit my spirit (Luke 23:46).*

- *Dear woman, here is your son . . . Here is your mother (John 19:26–27).*

- *I am thirsty (John 19:28).*

- *It is finished (John 19:30).*

Jesus Is Risen!

- Jesus returned to earth after he was resurrected and appeared a number of different times. How many of these appearances were recorded in the Bible? Eleven times. He appeared to:

Mary Magdalene *(Mark 16:9).*
The women at the tomb *(Matthew 28:9).*
Two people on the road *(Luke 24:13–35).*
Ten of his disciples *(John 20:19–20).*
Eleven disciples with Thomas *(John 20:26).*
Peter and a crowd of five hundred people *(1 Corinthians 15:6).*
Seven disciples when fishing *(John 21:1–14).*
Eleven disciples on the mountain *(Matthew 28:16–17).*
Jesus's brother, James *(1 Corinthians 15:7).*
The people who watched him ascend into heaven *(Luke 24:51; Acts 1:9).*
Paul *(1 Corinthians 15:8).*

The Traditions of Easter and Lent

- **What is Lent?** Lent is a church season during which people pray and prepare to celebrate Easter.

- **When does Lent begin?** On Ash Wednesday, the fortieth day before Easter.

- **Why did people wave palm branches when Jesus rode by?** The people welcomed Jesus for a festive occasion. Today, the church celebrates that day as Palm Sunday.

- **What does Easter celebrate?** The resurrection of Jesus Christ.

- **Whose idea was it to color eggs?** The ancient Egyptians, Greeks, Romans, and Persians celebrated spring by coloring beautiful eggs because they were a symbol of new life and fertility.

- **Why boiled eggs?** During the time of Lent, people were forbidden to eat eggs. So when Easter arrived, everyone was ready to dig in and eat them once again!

- **Why do we get all dressed up on Easter?** New beginnings have a long-time tradition in casting off the old and bringing in the new!

An Easter Carol

(A VeggieTales video)

- **What was Mr. Nezzer going to build in order to keep Easter year round?** EasterLand.

- **What does the minister do when Mr. Nezzer unveils his plans for EasterLand?** He faints.

- **What VeggieTales villain steals the orphan's pencils on the street?** Charlie Pincher.

- **What does Cavis do as soon as he gets out of the egg cart that rescued him from the Easter Egg Factory?** He kisses the ground.

- **What falls from the sky at the very end of the VeggieTales show *An Easter Carol*?** Plastic Easter eggs.

WRITING THE BIBLE

In the beginning was the Word, and the Word was with God, and the Word was God (John 1:1).

God as Creator

- **How long did it take to write the Bible?** Over 1,500 years!

- **How long ago was the Bible written?** The Old Testament was completed 2,400 years ago. The New Testament was completed 1,900 years ago.

- **What was the Bible written on?** On papyrus (made from reeds) or parchment (made from animal skins).

- **Can you name a book found in the very first library?** Sure you can—the Bible!

- **How many different people wrote the Bible?** Forty.

Larry sings, "Oh Where Is My Hairbrush?"

What kinds of people wrote the Bible?

Shepherds, farmers, kings, tent makers, physicians, philosophers, fishermen, and disciples of Jesus.

- Who took all those books and put the Bible together?
Scribes took ancient copies of each book to put together the Bible. Each time a scribe sat down to make a copy of the Bible, the process went like this:
  - He would read the sentence he was about to copy.
  - Then he would read it again out loud.
  - Then he would write the sentence.
  - After finishing a copy of a book, he would count all the words and letters in his copy and in the original book to be certain they were the same.
  - Then the scribe would find the middle word and the middle letter of each copy to make certain he had not made any mistakes.

Writing VeggieTales

- The most popular silly song ever, as voted by our fans, is "The Hairbrush Song." Did you know that Mike Nawrocki was inspired to write "The Hairbrush Song" one morning when he could not find his razor in the bathroom?

- What was the original title of the VeggieTales show *Duke and the Great Pie War*? *Princess and the Pie War.*

- When *Jonah–a VeggieTales Movie* was being created, there was one character besides Archibald Asparagus who was being considered for the title role of Jonah. Who was it? Jimmy Gourd.

- In the catacombs, Minnesota Cuke finds some paintings on the walls. The paintings depict the story of Samson. Which Veggie character is Samson? The Peach. Because he's got hair.

59

THE FASCINATING LIBRARY OF BOOKS BETWEEN TWO COVERS

• In the Bible how many . . .

Books? 66. Chapters? 1,189. Verses? 31,101.
Words? 783,187. Letters? 5,566,480. (KJV)

• **How many major divisions are there in the Bible?** The 66 books of the Bible are divided into two major sections: the Old Testament with 39 books and the New Testament with 27 books.

What different kinds of books are found in the Bible? In those two sections, you will find:

• **Books of Law**—The first five books are called the Pentateuch, which means "five scrolls."
• **Books of Old Testament History**—The next twelve books.
• **Books of Poetry and Wisdom**—The next five books are books of poetry, wisdom, drama, worship, and even a love song.
• **Books of the Prophets**—The last seventeen books of the Old Testament include stories about the prophets (12 major prophets and 5 minor prophets) who preached important messages from God to his people.

• **The Gospels**—The first four books of the New Testament share the story of Jesus and are recorded by four eyewitnesses to the events that took place. Two of the gospel writers, Matthew and John, were part of Jesus's twelve apostles. The word *gospel* means "good news."
• **Book of History**—The Book of Acts records the beginning of Jesus's church and teachings of the apostles to the early Christians.
• **The Letters**—The next twenty-one books are a collection of letters written by Christian leaders to the very first churches.
• **Revelation**—Just one book includes a series of visions of the future, written to encourage Christians toward their faith in God.

- **How many households in America own a Bible?** It is estimated that 90 percent of American households have owned a Bible at some time or another.

- **How many read the Bible? Well, that's a different story.** Only 31 percent of the people who own a Bible supposedly read it!

- **How many times does the word *Bible* appear in the Bible?** None!

- **So where does the word *Bible* come from?** It comes from the Latin word *biblia*, which means "book."

- **When was the first English Bible translated?** In 1382, by John Wycliffe.

- **How many different people are mentioned in the Bible?** 2,930.

- **So how does the Bible apply to you?** *All Scripture is God-breathed and is useful for teaching, rebuking, correcting and training in righteousness, so that the man of God may be thoroughly equipped for every good work (2 Timothy 3:16–17).*

A Big Idea from the Bible

- **How many VeggieTales shows are based on stories from the Bible?** 12.

- **What are they?**
  Duke and the Great Pie War: Ruth and Naomi.
  The Story of Flibber-o-loo: The Good Samaritan.
  The Star of Christmas: The birth of Jesus.
  Daniel and the Lions' Den: Daniel.
  Rack, Shack and Benny: Shadrach, Meshach and Abednego.
  Josh and the Big Wall: Joshua and the Battle of Jericho.
  Babysitter in DeNile: Miriam and Moses.
  King George and the Ducky: King David.
  The Ballad of Little Joe: Joseph.
  Jonah–a VeggieTales Movie: Jonah.
  Dave and the Giant Pickle: David and Goliath.
  Esther: The Girl Who Became Queen: Esther.

BIBLE FACTS & FIGURES

*More than 20 million Bibles are sold every year in the United States.
That doesn't count how many are given away for free!*

*The Bible has been translated in over 2,287 languages,
but it was originally written in just two: Hebrew and Greek.
In 2004, 21 languages were added!*

Bible lengths . . .

- **Most chapters:** Psalms.
- **Shortest book:** 3 John with 294 words, 14 verses. 2 John has 1 less verse but 4 more words (KJV).
- **Longest chapter:** Psalm 119.
- **Shortest chapter:** Psalm 117.
- **Longest verse:** Esther 8:9.
- **Shortest verses:** John 11:35—"Jesus wept." And Job 3:2—"He said."
- **The middle verse of the Bible:** Psalm 118:8.

- The following verses contain every letter in the entire alphabet except which ones? Ezra 7:21: The letters B, J, & Q. Daniel 4:37: The letter Q.

- It took three years of printing to create the very first copy of the Gutenberg Bible which was completed in 1455. It totaled 1,282 pages and had to be printed in two volumes. Almost two hundred originals were printed at that time and forty-eight of them still exist today.

- **What book of the Bible parallels the entire Bible itself?** Isaiah. **Why?** It has 66 chapters (the Bible has 66 books). The first 39 chapters deal with Israel (the first 39 books of the Bible do too).

- How many promises were made in the Bible? 1,260.

- How many prophecies were fulfilled? 3,268.

Interesting
Veggie Facts . . .

- In the first VeggieTales show, *Where's God When I'm S-Scared?* how old does Junior say he is in *Tales from the Crisper?* Five.

- Name the three villains that LarryBoy has faced? The Fib from Outer Space, The Rumor Weed, The Bad Apple.

- In the show *LarryBoy and the Fib from Outer Space*, what film is playing at the movie theater? *Invasion of the Cow Snatchers.*

- In the Larry-Mobile, what does the blue button turn on? Wipers. What does the green button do? Sounds the horn. What does the yellow button do? Turns the Larry-Mobile into the Larry-Plane.

- In the show *Madame Blueberry*, what kind of vehicle does Larry drive onto the countertop? Suzy Action Jeep. What color is it? Pink.

OLD TESTAMENT HEROES

For everything that was written in the past was written to teach us, so that through endurance and the encouragement of the Scriptures we might have hope (Romans 15:4).

The Many Stories of the Bible

The Bible is filled with great stories that help God's people to learn, grow, and understand all about God and their faith in him. Here are just some of the great heroes and adventures from the Bible. Test your knowledge and see how much you know about them!

Noah

• What did God ask Noah to do? Build a big boat, called an ark, and bring in every kind of creature from the earth—both male and female *(Genesis 6:13–21).*

• How long did God make it rain, and how long was the earth flooded? It rained for forty days and forty nights and the earth was flooded for 150 days *(Genesis 7:11–12, 24).*

• How old was Noah when the rain began? 600 years old *(Genesis 7:6, 11).*

• What kind of a sign did God give as a promise that he would never again flood the earth to destroy all the people? A rainbow *(Genesis 9:12–16).*

Abraham

• What did God tell Abraham he would become? Father of many nations *(Genesis 17:4).*

• What did God give to Abraham when he was 100 and Sarah when she was 90? A son, Isaac *(Genesis 21:1–6).*

• What is the test of faith that God gave to Abraham? God asked Abraham to sacrifice his son *(Genesis 22:1–11).*

• What did God do when Abraham responded in obedience? God allowed Abraham to spare his son *(Genesis 22:12–19).*

Joseph

- What did Joseph's father create for him because he was loved more? A coat with many colors *(Genesis 37:3)*.

- What ability did God give Joseph to help people in a very special way? God helped Joseph to interpret dreams *(Genesis 40)*.

- What did the Pharaoh's dream mean? Pharaoh's dream meant that there would be seven years of feast and then seven years of famine in the land *(Genesis 41:25–27)*.

- How did Joseph respond to his brothers when he saw them again during the years of famine? Joseph forgave his brothers *(Genesis 43—45)*.

A Rootin' Tootin' Bible Story

VeGGie Fun!

- In the VeggieTales story, *The Ballad of Little Joe*, Little Joe's father gave him a beautiful vest for his birthday. This was quite a departure from the mittens his brothers got for their birthdays. Where did his brothers keep their mittens? They hung them on the moose over the fireplace.

- Which of Little Joe's eleven brothers wears the black hat? Jude.

- There's a welcome sign at the entrance to Dodgeball City. What is the slogan at the bottom of the sign? Play Fair or Yer Out!

More OLD TESTAMENT HEROES

Moses

- **How did Moses get his name?** The Egyptian princess found the baby floating in the river and decided to raise him as her own. She called him Moses because it means to be lifted out of the water *(Exodus 2:1–10)*.

- **How did Moses get the message that he was to lead the people out of Egypt?** God spoke to him through the flames of a fire from within a bush that didn't burn *(Exodus 3:1–10)*.

- **Where did God lead Moses and the Israelites when they left Egypt?** He led them out of Egypt and around the desert road toward the Red Sea *(Exodus 14: 17–18)*.

- **What did Moses receive on Mount Sinai after he led the Israelites out of Egypt?** The Ten Commandments *(Exodus 19:20—20:17)*.

- **How many years did the Israelites wander in the desert?** Forty *(Deuteronomy 8:2)*.

- **Did Moses get to go into the promised land?** No. **Why?** Because he disobeyed God *(Exodus 20:7–11; Deuteronomy 3:23–29)*.

Joshua

- **God made Joshua the leader of the Israelites in place of a really great leader. Who did Joshua replace?** Joshua took Moses's place to lead the Israelites *(Deuteronomy 31:14; Joshua 1:1–2)*.

- **Moses had sent Joshua out as one of the twelve spies to do what?** Check out the Promised Land. *(Numbers 13: 16–17; Joshua 14:7)*.

- **How old was Joshua when he took over for Moses?** Almost ninety years old *(Deuteronomy 34; Joshua 24:29)*.

- **When the walls came down and Joshua and the Israelites overtook Jericho, one family was saved by placing a red ribbon outside their window. Who was that?** Rahab's family *(Joshua 2:17–21; 6:23)*.

Gideon

- **Who did Gideon have to fight? How many? And why?** Gideon is considered to be a great warrior. He defeated 120,000 Midianites, because they were taking anything they wanted from the Israelites' homes and farms. The Israelites didn't know what to do to stop them.

- **Gideon started out with 32,000 Israelites to fight against the Midianites. But God told him that he had too many men. What did Gideon do to reduce the number?** He let the men who were afraid go home. *(Judges 7).*

- **What did he use to fight this battle?** Only three hundred men with three hundred trumpets plus a great big God! *(Judges 7:19–22).*

- **What did Gideon also do to honor God?** He tore down the altars of Baal and built an altar to the one true God *(Judges 6:25–32).*

Keep Walkin'

- In the story *Josh and the Big Wall*, what Veggie character plays the Commander of the Army of the Lord? Archibald Asparagus.

- From on top of the big wall, Jean Claude and Phillipe make fun of Josh. What do they say? "You are not a mighty dill, you are just a baby gherkin!"

- Jimmy and Jerry build a crazy contraption in an effort to knock down the walls of Jericho. What is the name of their invention? The Wall-Minator 3000.

- In the story *Josh and the Big Wall*, what is on the menu in the Promised Land? Cheese soufflé, tacos, pintos and cheese, waffles and milk and honey.

Even More OLD TESTAMENT HEROES

Samuel

- How did Samuel get his name? His mother, Hannah, named him that and said, "Because I asked the LORD for him" *(1 Samuel 1:20)*.

- Who did Samuel learn from? Eli *(1 Samuel 3:1)*.

- Who called to Samuel during the night? God *(1 Samuel 3:4–11)*.

- The prophet Samuel anointed what two kings of Israel? King Saul *(1 Samuel 10:1)* and King David *(1 Samuel 16:13)*.

David

- For more than two hundred years, the Israelites had been fighting the Philistines. The Philistines issued a "giant" challenge to King Saul and the Israelites. What was it? Goliath, a giant Philistine, over nine feet tall, challenged any one Israelite to fight him *(1 Samuel 17:18–11)*.

More about David

- Who finally agreed to fight Goliath? David, a shepherd boy *(1 Samuel 17:45–50)*.

- Why did David think he could beat Goliath when all the other soldiers were afraid? He knew he had God on his side *(1 Samuel 17:34–37, 46–47)*.

- What did David take to fight against Goliath? A staff, five smooth stones, and a sling *(1 Samuel 17:40)*.

- After David killed Goliath, what did he become? A soldier in Saul's army *(1 Samuel 18:5)*.

- David wrote many songs to God. What are David's songs called? Psalms.

- What did God call David? A man after God's own heart *(Acts 13:22)*.

Samson

- What was the great gift that God blessed Samson with? Extraordinary strength *(Judges 16:5)*.

- Who did Samson fall in love with who later tried to trick him into finding out how he got his great strength? Delilah *(Judges 16:4–6)*.

- What did Samson tell Delilah was the source of his strength? Samson misled Delilah three times, but then confessed that he got his strength from never having had his hair cut *(Judges 16:17)*.

Job

- To whom did God brag about the blameless, upright character of Job? Satan *(Job 1:8)*.

- Satan didn't like the fact that Job was such an honorable child of God. So what did God allow Satan to do? God allowed Satan to test Job by bringing many different hardships to his life *(Job 1–2)*.

- How did Job respond to the test? Job remained true to God and his faith, despite everything that happened to him *(Job 42:8)*.

- How did God reward Job for his faithfulness? God gave Job twice as much as he had before *(Job 42:10)*.

In a Pickle

- In the story *Dave and the Giant Pickle*, what snack did Dave bring to his brothers on the battlefield? Pizza . . . with cheese in the crust.

- In the Veggie story *Dave and the Giant Pickle*, when Dave doesn't want to pick up his brothers' sheep, they remind him of the time they dipped him in tar and stuck him to what? The backside of an angry water buffalo.

Junior as Dave in *Dave and the Giant Pickle*.

69

Yep, There's More

OLD TESTAMENT HEROES

Daniel

- Daniel served King Darius and was one of the king's favorites. This made other men who worked for the king jealous. How did they seek revenge toward Daniel? They convinced the king to make a decree that, for the next thirty days, anyone who prayed to any god or man, except the king, would be punished (*Daniel 6:6–7*).

- Daniel continued to pray to God, because he knew it was the right thing to do. What was his punishment for doing this? He was thrown into the lions' den (*Daniel 6:16*).

- What did God do to the lions? He sent an angel who shut the mouths of the lions so they could not hurt Daniel (*Daniel 6:22*).

- How did Daniel's belief in God affect the king? The king and all the people began to believe in God too (*Daniel 6:26–27*).

Shadrach, Meshach, and Abednego

- Shadrach, Meshach, and Abednego worked for King Nebuchadnezzar. But the king created a huge golden statue of himself. He told everyone to bow down to the statue and worship it. What did Shadrach, Meshach, and Abednego do? They would not worship the golden image the king created (*Daniel 3:12*).

- What was their punishment? The king put them into a hot, fiery furnace (*Daniel 3:19–21*).

- What did the king see when he looked into the furnace to see what was happening? There were four men walking around in the fire, instead of three. (The fourth person was Jesus there with them). Then Shadrach, Meshach, and Abednego came out of the furnace, unharmed (*Daniel 3:25–27*).

Jonah

- When God told Jonah to go to Nineveh and tell them to stop disobeying him, what did Jonah do instead? He went on board a ship headed in the opposite direction (*Jonah 1:3*).

- How did God show his anger for Jonah? God sent a huge storm that almost made the ship sink (*Jonah 1:4*).

- What happened after Jonah confessed his wrong? He told the men to throw him overboard and the sea would be calm again. After they did, he was swallowed up by a big fish (*Jonah 1:12–17*).

- How long was Jonah in that fish? For three days until he was spit back out on dry land (*Jonah 1:17—2:10*).

- Then what did Jonah do? He obeyed God and went to Nineveh (*Jonah 3:3*).

VeggieFun!

Mr. Lunt keeps employees in line at the Chocolate Factory!

- In the Veggie story *Rack, Shack and Benny*, what are the hours for the employees at the Nezzer Chocolate Factory? They start at 8:00 and they don't get lunch 'til 3:00.

- At the beginning of the show, one employee of the chocolate factory has an injury. What is it? He has an anvil on his head.

The Bunny … The Bunny … Oh, I Love the Bunny!

- What does Mr. Lunt tell him to do about it? Get back on the line, you'll be just fine.

- In the chocolate factory, where do all the bad bunnies go? The furnace. According to Mr. Nezzer, whoever doesn't bow down and sing the Bunny Song is a what? A bad bunny.

NEW TESTAMENT

The New Testament stories are found in two categories: 1) the Gospels which record the life, death, and resurrection of Jesus Christ; and 2) the new church and the spreading of the gospel messages

Jesus

- Each of the Gospels tells something different about Jesus. Can you name the Gospels? Matthew, Mark, Luke, and John.

- Who was Jesus? God's Son *(Matthew 3:17).*

- Why did Jesus come to earth? To save us from our sins and give us eternal life *(John 3:16).*

- More than anyone else, Jesus does what? Loves you! *(Romans 8:38).*

You can find a great deal more information about Jesus in other sections of this book.

John

- Who was John's (the disciple) brother, and what was their occupation? John's brother was James, and they were fishermen *(Matthew 4:21).*

- How did John refer to himself in his Gospel? The disciple whom Jesus loved *(John 13:23; 19:26; 20:2; 21:7, 20).*

- What event did John, Peter, and James experience with Jesus when his "face shone like the sun and his clothes became as white as the light?" The transfiguration *(Matthew 17:1–2).*

- How does John act toward Jesus after Judas's betrayal? John follows Jesus boldly to his trial *(John 18:15–16)* and again to his crucifixion *(John 19:26–27).*

- **In what circumstance did Jesus invite Peter to show his faith?** Jesus asked Peter to come to him when he was walking on the water *(Matthew 14:27–29)*.

- **When Jesus predicted his death, what was Peter's response?** He told Jesus that it would never happen *(Matthew 16:22)*.

- **What question about forgiveness did Peter ask Jesus?** He asked Jesus if he should forgive others up to seven times. Jesus responded by saying, "I tell you, not seven times, but seventy-seven times" *(Matthew 18:21–22)*.

- **What does Jesus tell Peter that he will do three times?** Jesus says Peter will tell others he doesn't know Jesus *(Matthew 26:34, 75)*.

A Friend Is a Friend Is a Friend

Aside from the great friendship between Bob and Larry, every VeggieTales show features a special friendship that helps us learn the lesson. Can you name some of them?

- *Where's God When I'm S-Scared* — Junior and his dad
- *The Gourds Must Be Crazy* — Jimmy and Jerry
- *The Story of Flibber-o-loo* — Junior and Larry
- *Rack, Shack and Benny* — Junior, Larry and Bob (Rack, Shack and Benny)
- *Jonah – a VeggieTales Movie* — Archibald and Khalil (Jonah and Khalil)
- *King George and the Ducky* — Larry and Bob (King George and Louis)
- *The Ballad of Little Joe* — Larry and his family (Little Joe and his family)
- *Minnesota Cuke and the Search for Samson's Hairbrush* — Larry and Petunia (Cuke and Julia)
- *Duke and the Great Pie War* — Larry and Petunia (Duke and Princess Petunia)
- *LarryBoy* — Larry and Archie (LarryBoy and Alfred)
- *Esther: The Girl Who Became Queen* — Esther and Pa Grape (Esther and Mordecai)
- *Madame Blueberry* — Madame Blueberry and her butlers (Bob and Larry)
- *An Easter Carol* — Mr. Nezzer and Hope

PAUL'S JOURNEYS

As ne neared Damascus on his journey, suddenly a light from heaven flashed around him. He fell to the ground and heard a voice say to him, "Saul, Saul, why do you persecute me?" "Who are you, Lord?" Saul asked. "I am Jesus, whom you are persecuting," he replied. "Now get up and go into the city, and you will be told what you must do" (Acts 9:3–6).

• **Do you know where Paul was born and grew up?** Paul was born in Tarsus as a Roman citizen *(Acts 28:3, 28–29)*.

• **How did Paul treat the Christians since he grew up as a Jew?** Paul was very active in persecuting the new Christians. He even helped when they were stoned *(Acts 7:58; 8:1)*; he threatened them *(Acts 9:1–2)*; and he helped take them to jail *(Acts 22:3–5)*.

• **Then what wonderful thing happened to Paul?** Jesus spoke to him and told him go on into the city of Damascus and someone would tell him what he should do *(Acts 9:4–6)*.

• **After Paul's conversion, how did some of the Christians react when he told them what happened?** They were afraid of him and didn't believe him *(Acts 9:26)*.

• **What was Paul's goal on his missionary journeys?** To preach the Good News about Jesus Christ *(1 Corinthians 15:1–4)*.

• **What did Paul and Silas do at midnight while they were in prison?** Prayed and sang hymns to God *(Acts 16:25)*.

• **What did God do while Paul and Silas were in jail?** God caused a big earthquake which opened the prison and loosed everyone's chains. But no one ran away. Instead, Paul and Silas stayed and helped the jailer to come to faith in Jesus *(Acts 16:26–34)*.

- When Paul was a prisoner on board a ship during a great storm what did he tell the sailors they had to do in order to make it safely to dry land? They had to stay with the ship, instead of abandoning it. Later Paul and the sailors did make it safely to shore (*Acts 27:30–31*).

- Paul wrote letters to the churches to help them learn more about Jesus. Some of those letters are used as New Testament books of the Bible. Can you name them? Romans, 1 and 2 Corinthians, Galatians, Ephesians, Philippians, Colossians, 1 and 2 Thessalonians, 1 and 2 Timothy, Titus, Philemon and possibly Hebrews.

Letters from the Countertop

Paul is known for the letters he wrote. Most VeggieTales shows start with a letter from a child who wants to ask Bob and Larry a question.

- What was the very first letter ever written to Bob and Larry? From Lucy Anderson of Phoenix, Arizona, who was scared of the monsters in her closet.

- At the beginning of *Lyle the Kindly Viking*, Bob notes that they have gotten lots of letters about sharing. What are the questions that Larry lists? When do I have to share? Why do I have to share? What ever happened to Sonny and Cher?

BIBLE TIME WAR

Praise be to the LORD my Rock, who trains my hands for war, my fingers for battle (Psalm 144:1).

What Does the Bible Say About War?

- The very first wars were initiated by God against the enemies of his people *(Exodus 17:16; Numbers 31:3)*.

- In the New Testament, Jesus taught that peace is better than war *(Matthew 5:38–45)*.

- Other New Testament writers reinforced Jesus's words and encouraged the people not to repay evil with evil *(Romans 12:17–21)*.

- What did God tell the Israelites to do before they went to war? To first offer peace *(Deuteronomy 20:10–12)*.

- Why did our country's founding leaders think that they could ask God to bless America? "Blessed is the nation whose God is the LORD" *(Psalm 33:12)*.

Weapons and Armor

- What was one of the deadliest weapons in Bible times? A slingshot!

- In Saul's day, slings were deadly weapons and not something young boys used as toys. Soldiers used slings in warfare *(Judges 20:16; 1 Chronicles 12:2)*. Also, the stones used weren't pebbles, but rocks that weighed as much as two pounds each. No wonder Goliath fell over dead when David hit him!

- Cities were captured in a variety of different ways during Bible times. Can you name some of them?

- **Fires** were built at the base of the city walls. The heat made the stones in the wall crack, and then the army could break through.
- **Catapults** shot huge boulders against the city walls or over the walls into the city.
- **Tunnels** were dug under the walls of the city so soldiers could sneak into the city and attack from the inside.
- **Ramps** were built against the city walls, and armies would go up the ramps and onto the tops of the walls. This is how Jerusalem was captured.

A Shout That Shook the City

God helped Joshua capture the city of Jericho, which was surrounded by giant walls that were highly guarded. God told Joshua to march around the city for six days with armed men; to have seven priests carry trumpets of rams' horns in front of the ark of the covenant. On the seventh day, they marched around the city seven times with priests blowing trumpets. When they gave a long blast, the entire army was to shout and the walls of the city would collapse and everyone could go in. Joshua followed God's orders and everything happened according to God's plan (*Joshua 6: 1–16, 20*).

The Armor of God

God gives *us* spiritual armor as power to stand against the devil's schemes (*Ephesians 6:10–18*).

Belt of truth
Breastplate of righteousness
Footgear to spread the gospel of peace
Shield of faith
Helmet of salvation
Sword of the Spirit, which is the **Word** of God

Veggie Battles

In the VeggieTales show *The Asparagus of La Mancha*, Don Quixote dreams of a battle where he is fighting an army of peas. What are the peas using as a weapon? They are flinging hamburgers at him with a spatula catapult.

Why won't anyone in the town listen to Alfred when he asks them to help LarryBoy fight the Rumor Weed? They all think he's a robot.

CRIME AND PUNISHMENT
Punishments long ago . . .

During Bible times it was a real "pain in the neck" to lose a battle because the winners often stood on the necks of the losers to show they had won the battle (Joshua 10:24).

Exodus, Leviticus, Numbers, and Deuteronomy list quite a few laws about crimes and punishment. Here are a few:

• **What should be done if someone deliberately kills another person?** The murderer should be put to death *(Exodus 21:12–14).*

• **What should happen if someone hurts another in a fight?** The person who hurt the other must pay the injured person for any time lost from work until he has healed *(Exodus 21:19).*

• **What should someone do if he steals from another?** He must pay back four or five times as much *(Exodus 22:1).*

• **How much should a man charge to borrow money?** Nothing if the borrower was a fellow Israelite *(Exodus 22:25).*

Ever feel bad about being sent to your room or getting grounded? Well the Bible talks about some really severe punishments!

The Punishment: Death
The Crime:
• Disobeying parents *(Deuteronomy 21:18–21).*
• Blaspheming—saying bad things about God *(Leviticus 24:13).*
• Breaking the Sabbath *(Numbers 15:32–36).*
• Witchcraft *(Exodus 22:18).*
• Worshiping idols *(Leviticus 20:2).*
• Murder *(Leviticus 24:17).*

The Punishment: Going to Prison
The Crime:
- Disobeying the law *(Ezra 7:26)*.

The Punishment: A fine
The Crime:
- Fighting or hurting others *(Exodus 21:22)*.
- Stealing animals *(Exodus 22:1–4)*.

The Punishment: A whipping
The Crime:
- Being found guilty in court of disputing with another person *(Deuteronomy 25:1–3)*.

The New Christians

The early Christians had bad things done to them because they believed in and told others about Jesus. This suffering is called persecution. Early followers of Christ were persecuted in various ways *(Luke 21:12)*.

- Can you name some of them? Stoning *(Acts 6)*, flogging *(Hebrews 11:36)*, imprisonment *(Acts 16:16–23)*, chaining *(Acts 12:6)*, death by sword *(Acts 12:2)*, death by beheading *(Matthew 14:1–12)*, being sawed in two *(Hebrews 11:37)*. Some Christians are still persecuted today!

- Who blamed Christians for the burning of Rome? Nero in AD 64.

More Veggie Battles

- Who sings: *"The battle is not ours. We look to God above. For he will guide us safely through and guard us with his love?"* Esther.

- In the VeggieTales show *King George and the Ducky*, what does King George do to get rid of Thomas so that he can have his duck? He sends him off to the Great Pie War.

79

CHILDREN, FAMILIES, AND TRADITIONS

Fix these words of mine in your hearts and minds; tie them as symbols on your hands and bind them on your foreheads. Teach them to your children, talking about them when you sit at home and when you walk along the road, when you lie down and when you get up. Write them on the doorframes of your houses and on your gates (Deuteronomy 11:18–20).

What were families like during Bible times?

- They were much larger as they had one father who had one wife or maybe even several wives, and a lot of children.

- The oldest man of the family was the head or patriarch, and he was in charge. When he died, his oldest son took over as head.

- Multiple families often lived together in just one house. Married daughters and their husbands and their children lived with their parents. Plus, there might be grandparents, aunts, uncles, cousins, slaves, foreigners staying with them, and guests.

- Children played, but they all had chores too. They had to take care of the livestock or work in the field.

- Girls didn't go to school as the boys did, but they were taught by their mothers how to take care of the family and home.

- It was the parents' responsibility to teach their children faith in God and prayer. Guess what—it still is!

- The firstborn Jewish son was to be the ruler of the family *(2 Chronicles 21:3)*; the spiritual head of the family *(Exodus 13:1, 2)*; and receive a double portion of the father's goods when the inheritance was divided *(Deuteronomy 21:15–17)*.

- Children were considered to be a gift from God *(Psalm 127)*. They still are!

 **Veggie Fun!**

Veggie Relations

- In the VeggieTales story *Duke and the Great Pie War*, how are Nona and Petunia related? Nona is Petunia's mother-in-law.

- How is Duke related to Nona? He's Nona's second cousin (twice removed).

- Who does Duke have to face in a jousting tournament, and how is his competition related to Nona? Otis the Elevated. He is Nona's brother-in-law.

- How is Gildersleeve related to Nona? He was her husband. He was creamed in the Great Pie War.

From *Duke and the Great Pie War*

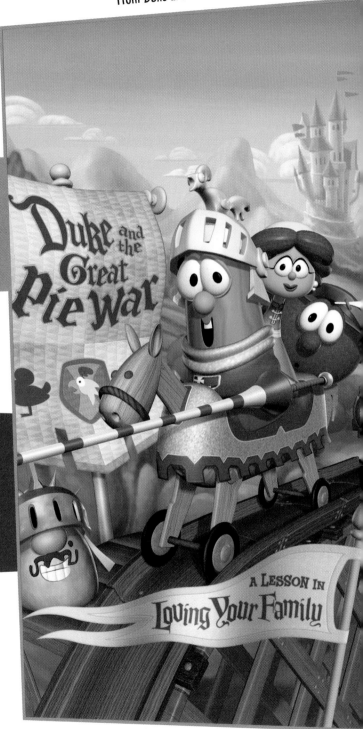

BIBLE TIME CHILDREN AND FAMILIES

Guess Who . . .

- was a shepherd boy who fought a giant and became a king? David (*1 Samuel 17*).

- were the first two people created? Adam and Eve (*Genesis 2:7–25*).

- was born in a manger in Bethlehem? Jesus (*Luke 2:1–7*).

- left Peter standing at the gate? Rhoda (*Acts 12:12–14*).

- had a brother who floated down a river as a baby? Miriam and Aaron (*Exodus 2:1–4*).

- was thrown in a well and sold by his brothers? Joseph (*Genesis 37:23–28*).

- were very young kings of Judah? Joash (7) (*2 Kings 11—12*); Josiah (8) (*2 Kings 22—23*); and Manasseh (12) (*2 Kings 21*).

- built a big boat and put lots of animals on it? Noah (*Genesis 6—7*).

- sold his birthright to his brother Jacob? Esau (Genesis 25:27–34).

- had a lunch that Jesus used to feed five thousand people? The boy with the loaves and fishes (*John 6:1–14*).

- lost his birthright due to his disobedience? Reuben was the firstborn son of Jacob, however, his brother Joseph received his birthright (*Genesis 49:1–4*).

- had a grandfather who lived to be the oldest man in the Bible, and how old did he live to be? Noah's grandfather, Methuselah, lived to be 969 years old (*Genesis 5:27*).

- had a nephew who saved his life when he overheard a plot to kill him? Paul (*Acts 23:12–24*).

- was a beautiful queen who risked her life to save the Jews? Esther (*Book of Esther*).

- was a boy who heard God speaking to him? Samuel (*1 Samuel 3*).

- had the first recorded fight between brothers? Cain and Abel (*Genesis 4:5–12*).

Some Well-Known Brothers and Sisters in the Bible

- Cain and Abel *(Genesis 4:1–12)*
- Esau and Jacob *(Genesis 25:24–26)*
- Joseph and his brothers (Genesis 37:4–20)
- Nadab and Abihu *(Leviticus 10:1)*
- Moses, Miriam, and Aaron *(Numbers 26:59)*
- Adonijah and Solomon *(1 Kings 1:5–30)*
- James and John *(Mark 10:35–40)*
- Peter and Andrew *(John 1:41)*
- Jesus and James *(Matthew 13:55)*
- James and John *(Matthew 14:18)*
- Mary, Martha, and Lazarus *(John 11:1–2)*

- In the VeggieTales story *Esther: The Girl Who Became Queen*, how is Mordecai related to Esther? They are cousins.

- Why can't Esther tell Haman that she is related to Mordecai? Because Haman hates her whole family.

26 . . . Count 'em!

- Who was Jesus's great, grandfather? King David *(Matthew 1)*.

- Whose wife was turned into a pillar of salt? Lot *(Genesis 19:26)*.

More Veggie Relations

- In *Esther: The Girl Who Became Queen*, what will happen to Esther's entire family? They will be banished to the Isle of Perpetual Tickling.

83

WHAT'S IN A NAME?

- What is the name of the very first woman, and what does her name mean? Eve—the mother of all the living *(Genesis 3:20)*.

- What is the most popular name for a man in the Bible? Zechariah. Thirty-one men had this name.

- In which books of the Bible does the word "God" *not* appear? Esther and Song of Solomon.

- How many times do these names appear? God: 4,170; Lord: 7,279; Jesus: 909; David: 1119; Moses: 803; Jacob: 362; Saul: 410; Aaron: 339; Abraham: 306; Solomon: 298; Joseph: 245; Paul: 298; Holy Spirit: 90.

- Who is the most talked about:
  –man in the Bible? Jesus—2,281 times
  –woman in the Bible? Sarah—56 times (KJV).

- How many different names was Jesus referred to in the entire Bible? Over one hundred!

- In how many books of the Bible was Jesus referred to? All of them!

- How many people were named Mary in the Bible? Seven of them: Mary, mother of Jesus *(Matthew 1:16)*; Mary Magdalene *(Matthew 27:56)*; Mary, mother of James and Joses *(Mark 15:40)*; Mary, wife of Clopas *(John 19:25)*; Mary, sister of Martha *(Luke 10:39)*; Mary, mother of John Mark *(Acts 12:12)*; Mary *(Romans 16:6)*.

- Joshua means "the Lord saves." How many people were named Joshua in the Bible? Twelve: Joshua, son of Nun, who was the leader after Moses *(Exodus 33:11)*; Joshua of Bethshemesh, on whose land the ark halted *(1 Samuel 6:14)*; Hoshea, son of Azaziah *(1 Chronicles 27:20)*; Joshua, governor of Jerusalem *(2 Kings 23:8)*; Hoshea, son of Elah, king of Israel *(2 Kings 15:30)*; Jeshua, a Levite in the time of King Hezekiah *(2 Chronicles 31:15)*; Jeshua, a Levite *(Ezra 2:40)*; Jeshua, father of Ezer *(Nehemiah 3:19)*; Jeshua, son of Kadmiel, a Levite *(Nehemiah 12:24)*; Hoshea, one of the "chiefs of the people" *(Nehemiah 10:23)*; Joshua, a high priest in the time of the prophet Zechariah *(Zechariah 3:1)*; Jesus is the Greek version of the Hebrew name Joshua. In Matthew 1:21, the angel told Joseph, "You are to give him the name Jesus, because he will save his people from their sins."

Popular Names

Here is a list of the most popular names today that are taken from Bible names or Bible words:

BOYS . . .
- Abraham
- Jacob
- Caleb
- Joshua
- Ethan
- Gabriel
- Joseph
- Jesus
- David
- Alexander
- Aaron
- Moses
- John
- Noah
- Saul
- Daniel
- Luke
- Michael
- Matthew
- Solomon
- Zachary
- Jonathan
- Samuel

GIRLS . . .
- Esther
- Eve
- Julia
- Judith
- Ruth
- Faith
- Hannah
- Danielle
- Jordan
- Elizabeth
- Rebecca
- Anna
- Leah
- Martha
- Tamar
- Grace
- Sarai
- Mary
- Abigail
- Naomi
- Chloe
- Sarah
- Gabrielle
- Rachel

VeGGie Fun!

What's in a Name?

- In the Silly Song *Love My Lips*, Larry meets a kid while he's in lip rehab. What is his name, and what happened to him? Oscar. He got stung by a bee right on the lips.

- In the Silly Song *Larry's High Silk Hat*, there's a character who says he's never been given a name. What kind of vegetable is he? A scallion.

ROYALTY

And David knew that the LORD had established him as king over Israel and had exalted his kingdom for the sake of his people Israel (2 Samuel 5:12).

Famous Kings from the Bible

- **What king had the shortest reign?** King Zimri, who ruled only seven days *(1 Kings 16:15).*

- **Who was Israel's first king?** Saul. Israel wanted to be like all the other countries around them, and they kept asking God for a king *(1 Samuel 8:19).* So God had Samuel anoint Saul as the king of Israel.

- **Was Saul a good king?** He started out as a good king *(1 Samuel 11),* but later on he trusted less in God and more in himself *(1 Samuel 13).* Eventually Saul turned away from God, and God had him replaced by David. Saul ruled for forty years.

- **Who is considered Israel's greatest and most loved king?** David. *(1 Samuel 16; 1 Kings 2:11).* He was the youngest son of Jesse of Bethlehem. He took care of his father's sheep and was anointed king by Samuel.

- **What instrument could David play?** The harp. In fact, he played the harp so well that when Saul was in a bad mood, just listening to David's music helped him to be in a good mood *(1 Samuel 16:18–23).*

- **Who was the vainest king?** Nebuchadnezzar—he set up a statue of gold that was ninety feet tall and nine feet wide *(Daniel 3:5).*

- **What kings began the custom of shaking hands?** The kings in Babylon.

- **What is a pharaoh?** "Pharaoh" was the title for an Egyptian king, often used in place of the king's actual name (like we use the title "President" today).

- **Who was the youngest king?** Joash, who became king when he was seven years old *(2 Kings 11:21).* The second youngest king was Josiah, who was eight years old *(2 Kings 22:1).*

Veggie Royalty!

VeGGie Fun!

Many VeggieTales characters have played kings, queens, or other varieties of royalty in our shows. Can you name some of them?

- Larry the Cucumber played King George in *King George and the Ducky,* and he played Duke Duke in *Duke and the Great Pie War.*
- Archibald Asparagus played King Saul in *Dave and the Giant Pickle* and King Darius in *Daniel and the Lions' Den.*

- Esther played herself in *Esther: The Girl Who Became Queen.*
- Princess Petunia played herself in *Duke and the Great Pie War.*
- Mr. Twisty played the king of Nineveh in *Jonah–a VeggieTales Movie.*
- Mr. Nezzer played King Xerxes in *Esther: The Girl Who Became Queen.*
- Miss Achmetha played the princess of Egypt in the *Babysitter in DeNile.*

Mr. Nezzer plays King Xerxes in *Esther: The Girl Who Became Queen.*

MORE ROYALTY

Solomon was King David's son who became king after his father. King Solomon was the wisest and the richest king who ever lived (1 Kings 3:11-14).

King Solomon's Kingly Numbers:

- 4,000 stalls for his horses *(1 Kings 4:26)*
- Daily food for his household— 185 bushels of flour, 375 bushes of meal, 10 oxen, 20 cattle, and 100 sheep and goats *(1 Kings 4:22–23)*
- 12,000 horses *(1 Kings 4:26)*
- wrote 3,000 proverbs *(1 Kings 4:32)*, Song of Solomon, and Ecclesiastes
- Composed 1,005 songs *(1 Kings 4:32)*
- 550 chief officers *(1 Kings 9:23)*
- Queen of Sheba gave Solomon 4 ½ tons of gold *(1 Kings 10:10)*
- Received 25 tons of gold in a year *(1 Kings 10:14)*
- 1,400 chariots *(1 Kings 10:26)*
- Had 700 wives *(1 Kings 11:3)*
- Had 300 concubines *(1 Kings 11:3)*
- Ruled over Israel for 40 years *(1 Kings 11:42)*

Famous Queens from the Bible

- Who was a Jewish girl who became queen of the Persian Empire because of her beauty? Esther. She was considered to be the most beautiful woman in all Persia, and God used her to save the Jewish people from being killed.

- How long did Esther take beauty treatments before she was allowed to go see the king of Persia? One year! *(Esther 2:12).*

- Who was a wicked queen and the opposite of Esther in every way? Jezebel. She and her husband, King Ahab, ruled over Israel during the time of Elijah.

- What was built for Jezebel's god? An altar to Baal *(1 Kings 16:29–32).*

- Who did Jezebel kill? All the prophets of God that she could *(1 Kings 18:4–13).*

Some Royal Veggie Fun

Bob as Louis in *King George and the Ducky*

- Who is King George's favorite general, and what VeggieTales character plays him? General Cedric played by a scallion.

- What is the name of the slightly odd wiseman who shows up at King George's door every so often to tell him things? Melvin.

- What does King George wear to disguise himself when he goes to steal Thomas's ducky? Funny glasses, nose, and moustache.

- What VeggieTales character plays Melvin? Pa Grape.

JUDGES

There were fourteen judges mentioned in the Bible.

- **How many were women?** Just one—Deborah. She was a wise woman and respected by the people. She would rule the people while she sat under a huge palm tree known as the Palm of Deborah (*Judges 4:5*). While she was a judge, Israel had peace for forty years.

The judges were leaders of Israel who not only judged the people but who were also military leaders expected to save the Israelites from their enemies. The judges are listed below:

1. Othneil . . . . *Judges 3:7–11:* ruled 40 years
2. Ehud . . . . *Judges 3:12–30:* ruled 80 years
3. Shamgar . . . . . . *Judges 3:31:* the Bible does not mention how long he ruled
4. Deborah . . . . . *Judges 4—5:* ruled 40 years
5. Gideon . . . . *Judges 6—8:* ruled 40 years
6. Tola . . . . *Judges 10:* ruled 23 years
7. Jair . . . . *Judges 10:3–5:* ruled 22 years
8. Jephthah . . . . . . *Judges 10:6–12:7:* ruled 6 years
9. Ibzan . . . . *Judges 12:8–10:* ruled 7 years
10. Elon . . . . *Judges 12:11–12:* ruled 10 years
11. Abdon . . . . *Judges 12:13–15:* ruled 8 years
12. Samson . . . . . . *Judges 13–16:* ruled 20 years
13. Eli . . . . *1 Samuel 4:18:* 40 years
14. Samuel . . . . *1 Samuel 7:15:* ruled all the days of his life

- Did Delilah cut Samson's hair? No! We often say that Delilah cut Samson's hair. But she did *not* cut his hair! Delilah learned that the secret of Samson's strength was his hair and she told Samson's enemies, the Philistines, and they cut his hair (*Judges 16:19*).

Khalil and The Pirates Who Don't Do Anything

YOU Be the Judge!

Veggie Fun!

- In *Jonah—a VeggieTales Movie*, Jonah, along with The Pirates Who Don't Do Anything and Khalil, are found guilty of what crime? High thievery against the royal city of Nineveh.

- What was their punishment? The Slap of No Return.

- Who is the king of Nineveh in *Jonah—a VeggieTales Movie*? King Twistomer.

- In the movie, what does Jonah say that causes the king to let them all go? He tells them that he had been in the belly of a whale.

- What does King Twistomer do to verify Jonah's story? He has the guard smell him.

91

APOSTLES

"Come follow me," Jesus said, "and I will make you fishers of men" (Matthew 4:19).

Who were the (twelve) very special men whom Jesus called to follow him in his ministry on earth?

1. Simon (Peter)—A fisherman by trade, he was one of three disciples closest to Jesus. Jesus named him Peter which means "rock." He was among the first to preach the gospel after Jesus was raised from the dead.

2. Andrew—A fishing partner of his brother, Peter, Andrew first believed in Jesus and then brought Peter to meet him.

3. James—James and his brother, John, were called "Sons of Thunder" by Jesus because they were so hot tempered.

4. John—James's brother. He was called "the disciple Jesus loved" because he was such a close friend of Jesus. He took care of Mary, Jesus's mother after Jesus's crucifixion. He wrote the books of John, 1, 2, and 3 John, and Revelation.

5. Philip—From the town of Bethsaida, this follower was known for his eagerness to introduce people to Jesus and brought Nathanael to Jesus.

6. Thomas—He showed his loyalty to Jesus by being willing to die with him. Later, however, he was named "Doubting Thomas" because he did not believe it when he was told that Jesus had been resurrected from the dead.

7. Matthew—He was a tax collector when he was called to follow Jesus. He wrote the Book of Matthew, the first Gospel of the New Testament.

8. Bartholomew (Nathanael)— He was from the town of Cana and was told about Jesus by Philip, and was with six other apostles when Jesus reappeared after his resurrection.

9. James (the lesser)—He was referred to as "the lesser" because he is younger than the other apostle James.

10. Thaddeus—His other name is Judas. There is only one record of him in the Gospels in addition to his being named as one of the Twelve, when he asked Jesus a question at the Last Supper.

11. Simon the Zealot—He was called a zealot because he wanted to turn against the Roman government.

12. Judas Iscariot—He was the treasurer for the apostles, and he betrayed Jesus with a kiss. When he realized what he had done, he killed himself.

Veggie Fishermen

- In *Jonah—a VeggieTales Movie,* what three kinds of leisure equipment do The Pirates Who Don't Do Anything shoot out of the cannon to try to get the whale to let Jonah go? A tennis racquet, two croquet mallets and a bowling ball.

- Who is hiding in the bowling ball? Khalil.

- Khalil has a nickname for Jonah that he uses when Jonah is being negative. What is the nickname? Mr. Grumpy-Pants.

PROPHETS

I will raise up for them a prophet like you from among their brothers: I will put my words in his mouth, and he will tell them everything I command him (Deuteronomy 18:18).

The Old Testament prophets were people who spoke the actual words of God to the Israelites, to help them turn away from worshiping idols and to turn back to God.

Major Prophets

- During that time there were false prophets who pretended that God told them to say certain things. Prophets were killed if they weren't 100 percent true in what they said (*Deuteronomy 13:1–5; 18:17–22*).

- The prophets in the Bible are divided into major and minor prophets, not because some were bigger or more important than the others, but because major prophets had longer books.

Above all, you must understand that no prophecy of Scripture came about by the prophet's own interpretation (2 Peter 1:20).

- Isaiah—Tells of the wonderful things about God (*Isaiah 5:16; 8:13; 12:2; 44:6*). He also writes about Jesus long before he was born (*Isaiah 7:14; 9:1–7; 11:1–12; 53:1–12*).

- Jeremiah—Called the weeping prophet because of his predictions for the bad things coming to Israel.

- **Ezekiel**—Went to the Valley of the Dry Bones and saw the bones of dead people come to life. This was a symbol of how God would bring the nation of Israel back to glory (*Ezekiel 37:1–14*).

- Daniel—Was put in a den of lions and saved by God. He received visions of what would happen in the future (*Daniel 2; 7; 8*).

Ebenezer Nezzer and Hope from *An Easter Carol*

An Easter Prophet

- In the VeggieTales show *An Easter Carol*, Ebenezer Nezzer is visited by a small but powerful "prophet." Who is it? Hope.

- What does Ebenezer think Hope is? A bug.

- What does Hope call Ebenezer? A first-class stinker.

- What is the message that Hope delivers? She explains the true meaning of Easter.

MINOR PROPHETS

*Above all, you must understand that no prophecy of Scripture came about
by the prophet's own interpretation (2 Peter 1:20).*

• Hosea—God has him marry a woman who isn't faithful to show the Israelites how they are acting toward God *(Hosea 1:1—3:5).*

• Joel—Warns of terrible punishments to come to the Israelites *(Joel 2:28—3:8).*

• Amos—Came to announce God's judgment *(Amos 1:1—2:16).*

• Obadiah—Preaches about the destruction of Edom in verses 1–14 and that God would once again bless the Israelites in verses 15–21.

• Jonah—Was swallowed by a great fish before he preached to people of Nineveh *(Jonah 1:1–2; 3:1–2).*

• Micah—Predicts that the Savior would be born in Bethlehem *(Micah 5:2).*

• Nahum—Wrote to comfort the people of Judah and tell them that their enemies' capital, Nineveh, would be destroyed. *(Nahum 2—3).*

• Habakkuk—Worked with godly King Josiah to turn the people of Judah toward God *(Habakkuk 1:3–4,6).*

• Zephaniah—Delivers a simple message to Judah that God is going to judge what they are doing *(Zephaniah 1:4).*

• Haggai—Preached sermons to get the Jews to finish building the temple *(Haggai 1:1–15).*

• Zechariah—Lived at the same time as Haggai and told the people of Judah that God would come again but it would not be soon *(Zechariah 14:5).*

• Malachi—Last book of the Old Testament; Malachi tells the people that God will punish the evil people, but those who obey Him will be rewarded *(Malachi 3:16–18).*

Name that Prophet!

Can you name the prophet who . . .

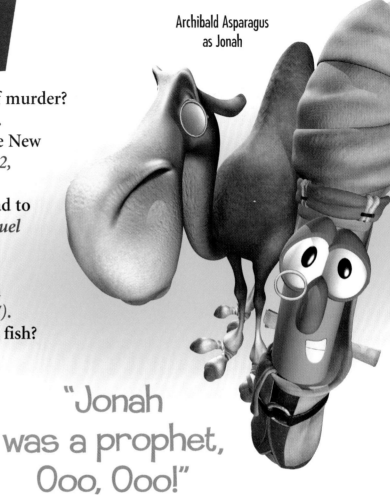

Archibald Asparagus
as Jonah

. . . accused King David of murder?
Nathan *(2 Samuel 12:1, 9)*.

. . . wrote five books in the New
Testament? John *(John; 1, 2,
3 John; Revelation)*.

. . . appeared from the dead to
King Saul? Samuel *(1 Samuel
28:15)*.

. . . was an eyewitness to
Jerusalem's ruin? Jeremiah
(Lamentations 2:13, 16–17).

. . . was swallowed by a big fish?
Jonah *(Jonah 1:17)*.

"Jonah was a prophet, Ooo, Ooo!"

- As the angel choir is singing inside the whale, there are two fishermen in a small rowboat on the surface of the water. Who were they? Scooter and George.

- What was the behavior problem of the Ninevites in the VeggieTales movie? They were fish slappers!

- The Veggies sing these lyrics: "Jonah was a prophet, ooo, ooo! But he never really got it! Sad but true!" What did Jonah not get? He never understood that God is all about compassion, mercy, and second chances. God wants us to respond to others that way too!

PEOPLE AND THEIR PROBLEMS

Everyone has problems! Some of the most famous people in the Bible certainly had their share. How many can you think of? Here are just some:

- Abraham was too old *(Genesis 17:17)*.

- Moses stuttered *(Exodus 4:10)*.

- Jacob was a liar *(Genesis 27)*.

- Gideon doubted *(Judges 6)*.

- Elijah was stressed out *(1 Kings 19:11–18)*.

- Solomon was too rich *(1 Kings 1:37)*.

- Joash was too young *(2 Kings 11:21)*.

- Jonah didn't like the job *(Jonah 1:3)*.

- Naomi was a widow *(Ruth 1:5)*.

- Peter was afraid of death *(Matthew 26:69–75)*.

- Thomas was a doubter *(John 20:25)*.

- Paul was a murderer *(Acts 8:1)*.

- Timothy had stomach trouble *(1 Timothy 5:22)*.

- Lazarus was dead *(John 11:11–17)*.

- Martha was a worry-wart *(Luke 10:41)*.

People, People, Everywhere!

(Estimates taken in 2005)
- Country with the smallest population: Vatican City: population 921.
- Country with the largest population: China: population 1,306,313,812.

- Population in America? 295,734,134.
- Largest city in the world? Tokyo: population 34,997,300.
- Largest nation of land? Russia has 6.5 million square miles of land.

- Poorest countries in the world: East Timor, Somalia, and Sierra Leone.
- Richest country in the world: Luxembourg.

Dad, Mom, and Junior Asparagus

Some Very Veggie Problems

- In *Bully Trouble*, Junior Asparagus dreams of being the star of a football team. In his dream, what is the final score of the game? 204 – 200.

Veggie Fun!

- What advice does Junior's dad give him about being bullied? He told Junior to face up to the bully.

- In *Going Up* on the video *Sumo of the Opera*, Larry the Cucumber, Jerry Gourd, and Mr. Lunt have a very big problem. What is it? They have to move a piano up a huge hill.

Finally, brothers, we instructed you how to live in order to please God, as in fact you are living. Now we ask you and urge you in the Lord Jesus to do this more and more. For you know what instructions we gave you by the authority of the Lord Jesus (1 Thessalonians 4:1–2).

BIBLE TIME FOODS AND MEALS

Then God said, "I give you every seed-bearing plant on the face of the whole earth and every tree that has fruit with seed in it. They will be yours for food (Genesis 1:29).

Can you name some of the foods that were eaten during Bible times?

- Barley—*(Ruth 2:23)*
- Bread—*(Luke 22:19)*
- Curds—*(Isaiah 7:22)*
- Cheese—*(1 Samuel 17:18)*

- Dates—*(2 Samuel 6:19)*
- Eggs—*(Job 6:6)*
- Figs—*(Numbers 13:23; 1 Samuel 25:18)*
- Fruits(All)—*(Genesis 1:29)*
- Grain—*(1 Samuel 17:17)*
- Grapes—*(Numbers 13:24)*
- Herbs (Leafy Plants) and Vegetables—*(Exodus 12:8; Daniel 1:12)*

- Honey—*(Deuteronomy 8:8)*
- Meats—(Beef, Fish, Lamb, Poultry, Venison) *(Leviticus 11; Deuteronomy 14)*
- Milk—*(Isaiah 7:21–22)*

- Nuts—*(Genesis 43:11)*
- Olives and Olive Oil—*(Deuteronomy 8:8; Ezekiel 16:19)*
- Salt—*(Leviticus 2:13)*
- Wheat (Bread, Cereal, Pasta)—*(Psalm 81:16)*

Let's Eat!

A day of meals in Bible times . . .

LATE BREAKFAST OR EARLY LUNCH:
- Some hollowed-out bread stuffed with cheeses, nuts, and vegetables. Maybe some fish and fruit.

LUNCH:
- Bread stuffed with cheeses, nuts, and vegetables. Maybe some fish.

DINNER:
- Fish, chicken, lamb, fowl, fruits, cheeses, nuts, vegetables, and soup. Desserts consisted of fruits, simple cookies, honey biscuits, cinnamon cakes, and honeycombs.

DRINK:
- Water, wine, goat's milk, and juices.

Fun Food Facts

- Who ate locusts and wild honey? Jesus's cousin, John the Baptist *(Matthew 3:4)*.
- Who discovered a very unusual snack in a very unusual place? Samson *(Judges 14:1–9)*.

VeGGie Fun!

- What prophet was fed by birds and ate bread baked by angels? Elijah *(1 Kings 17:6)*.
- What two nuts are mentioned in the Bible? Almonds and pistachios *(Genesis 43:11)*.

During 300 BC, cookies were first made in Rome. Because Jesus grew up in a land ruled by the Romans, he probably ate cookies as a boy.

Incoming Meteors and Other Foods!

- What Veggies ate a giant meteor to save their spaceship? Jimmy and Jerry Gourd. What was the meteor made out of? Popcorn.

- In *King George and the Ducky*, when Thomas returns from the Great Pie War, he is covered in what kind of pie? Boysenberry.

- What icy beverage do the peas who are on the wall throw on the Israelites to keep them away? Purple slushie.

MORE FUN FOOD FACTS

Did you know . . .

• **Who invented pancakes?** The Egyptians did, in 2600 BC. They were most likely made of goat's milk or water and mixed with some type of ground meal. But you had to wait for syrup until 1000 BC!

• Watermelons were first grown in Africa around the time that Jacob and Esau were born. Ice cream was invented in China about the same time, and bananas were cultivated in India.

• **Guess where spaghetti was first made?** Nope, it wasn't Italy! Pasta was first made in China around the time of King David.

• **What kinds of food did the ancient Greeks eat?** They grew olives, grapes, and figs. They kept goats for milk and cheese. They also grew wheat to make bread. Fish, seafood, and wine were very popular foods too. In larger cities, meat could be purchased, but it was rarely eaten. It was used primarily for religious sacrifices.

• **What did the Hebrews eat while in the desert for forty years?** Manna that fell from the sky! *(Exodus 16:4)*.

• **What person could have been a meal for a big fish?** Jonah, the prophet (although the fish spit him out) *(Jonah 1:17; 2:10)*.

• **What tax collector did Jesus forgive and then share a meal with?** Zacchaeus *(Luke 19:1–9)*.

Scene from *Going Up*

VeggieFun!

Pie Wars!

- In *Madame Blueberry*, what kind of food does Annie thank God for in the *Thankfulness Song*? Her piece of apple pie.

- In *Going Up* which two VeggieTales characters take a break from their moving job and eat an ice cream cone? Jerry Gourd and Mr. Lunt.

- In the show *The Ballad of Little Joe*, Little Joe's brothers make him a birthday cake. What frosted animal is on the cake? A cow.

- In the *Ultimate Silly Song Countdown*, The Pirates Who Don't Do Anything sing a brand-new Silly Song about what kind of food? Chinese food. What is the name of the song? "Do the Mooshoo."

BIBLE TIME CLOTHING

Your beauty should not come from outward adornment, such as braided hair and the wearing of gold jewelry and fine clothes. Instead, it should be that of your inner self, the unfading beauty of a gentle and quiet spirit, which is of great worth in God's sight (1 Peter 3:3–4).

• What was the very first clothing mentioned in the Bible? Fig leaves *(Genesis 3:7)*.

• What did God give Adam and Eve to wear? **Animal skins** *(Genesis 3:21)*.

What kinds of clothing did women wear in Bible times?

• Women wore long gowns with fringed or pointed sleeves. To keep warm, they would wear jackets, shawls, and scarves. Many times their clothes were decorated with lovely jewels, silver, or gold.

• What about soldiers? Soldiers wore a cloth girdle that was held up by leather shoulder straps that held their swords. They also wore helmets.

• What were clothes made out of in Bible times? Cotton, wool, and silk, which were available in lots of colors.

What kinds of clothing did the men wear in Bible times?

• Men also wore long gowns, but these were called tunics, often tied at the waist by a leather sash or cloth tie. To keep warm, they wore large cloaks, headscarves, or turbans.

• Did people wear shoes in Bible times? **Of course! They did a lot of walking, so shoes were often made of various leathers, especially sandals. Some shoes were also made of wood, palm-tree bark, or cane. The leather was wrapped around these materials and then tied to the feet with leather strings.**

- Did men and women wear any jewelry? Yes! Both men and women wore necklaces, bracelets, pins, barrettes, and earrings. Jewelry was made from various jewels, glass, ivory, gold, and silver. Even camels were known to wear jeweled chains!

Jimmy Gourd plays a character who lives in Flibber-o-loo.

- In the show *Rack, Shack and Benny*, the factory workers wear white caps. What is on the caps? A picture of a bunny.

- In the show *The Ballad of Little Joe*, what does Little Joe wear on his head while working at the Rootin' Tootin' Pizza Place? **A costume cow hat.**

- Makeup dates all the way back to Bible times when women wore various eye, lip, and cheek colors.

- Did people have their hair done? Yes! Women helped each other fix their hair. Women weren't allowed to wear their hair down in public. Instead, women's hair had to be tied back, braided, or covered with a headdress. Hebrew and Arab men had much longer hair and beards. But Egyptian men shaved their beards and sometimes their heads.

What Do Veggies Wear?

- What famous berry has been known to switch her hair from brown to blonde? Madame Blueberry.

- In *The Story of Flibber-o-loo* what did the Flibbians wear on their heads? Shoes. In Jibberty-lot they wore pots.

BIBLE TIME EDUCATION

Love the LORD your God with all your heart and with all your soul and with all your strength. These commandments that I give you today are to be upon your hearts. Impress them on your children. Talk about them when you sit at home and when you walk along the road, when you lie down and when you get up. Tie them as symbols on your hands and bind them on your foreheads. Write them on the doorframes of your houses and on your gates (Deuteronomy 6:5–9).

- **What was it like to go to school back in Bible times?** The very first children were taught at home *(Deuteronomy 6:6–7)*. Girls were raised to take care of the home, and only boys were educated. Between the years of Old and New Testament times, schools included both boys and girls in Rome. Boys usually received the most education.

How old were kids when they started school?

- At five or six, boys and girls started going to an elementary school called *bet sefer*. Although boys continued until they were fifteen if they displayed unusual ability, the girls were usually married by that age. Students attended school in the synagogue and were taught by the *hazzan* or a local Torah teacher. They learned the Torah through memorization.

- After the great flood of Noah, boys-only schools were set up by the Sumerians. They used clay tablets to write on. School started in the early morning hours and lasted until late evening. Clay tablets were replaced by leather scrolls during Elisha's time.

- During Greek civilization, boys went to school until they were 20 and then left for military service. In Athens, boys would serve in the military for only a few years, but in Sparta they served in the military until they were 60 years old.

- About 1700 BC, the first Western alphabet was invented in Phoenicia. From this alphabet, other nations made up their own methods of writing. This first alphabet had twenty-two letters and stood for simple sounds, rather than whole words. Later, the Greeks took that alphabet and developed letters so simple that more people learned to read and write.

What was school like for Jesus?

- Jesus often quoted from the Scriptures in his teachings, so he studied quite well! Jesus referred to sixteen different books of the Bible in his teachings.
- Jesus went to the synagogue every week. This was a place where the people went to worship God.
- Jesus's earthly dad, Joseph, was a carpenter, so he would have been taught the same trade as his father *(Matthew 13:55; Mark 6:3)*.

God Has a Lot to Say in His Book!

- In the show *The Toy That Saved Christmas*, Buzz-Saw Louie sings, "There must be more to Christmas." What does he eventually learn about Christmas? That it's not about getting; it's about giving.

- At the end of each VeggieTales show, Bob and Larry sum up the lesson with the help of a computer. What is the computer's name? QWERTY.

- In the show *King George and the Ducky*, King George sums up the lesson by singing what? "Being selfish doesn't pay. I tried it just the other day. I wanted to be happy. I thought it was the way. But it weren't."

- In *An Easter Carol*, through what vehicle does Hope teach Ebenezer Nezzer the lesson. She uses the stained-glass windows at the church.

BIBLE TIME WORK

Whistle While You Work!

- What were some of the very first jobs? Farmers and shepherds.

As populations increased, more jobs became needed, such as teachers, soldiers, doctors, lawyers, and money collectors. The first policemen and firemen worked for Caesar Augustus during the time of Jesus's boyhood.

- How many different jobs are noted in the Bible? 191!

Here is a list of just some of the Bible-time jobs:

- Farmer—*(Isaiah 28:24)*
- Shepherd—*(1 Samuel 17:20)*
- Business man—*(Genesis 13:2)*
- Butler (cupbearer)—*(Genesis 40:1)*
- Baker—*(Genesis 40:1)*

- Brick maker—*(Genesis 11:3)*
- Chariot driver—*(1 Kings 22:34)*
- Jeweler—*(Exodus 28:11)*
- Scribe—*(1 Chronicles 24:6)*

- Weaver—*(Exodus 35:35)*
- Teacher—*(Proverbs 5:13)*
- Councilman—*(Mark 15:43)*
- Lawyer—*(Acts 24:1)*
- Fisherman—*(Matthew 4:18)*

- Tentmaker—*(Acts 18:3)*
- Seamstress—*(Acts 9:39)*
- Cattleman—*(Genesis 4:19)*
- Blacksmith—*(1 Samuel 13:19)*
- Soldier—*(Acts 12:4)*
- Archer—*(Genesis 21:20)*
- Judge—*(Judges 2:18)*
- Carpenter—*(Matthew 13:55)*
- Doctor—*(Colossians 4:14)*

- Tax collector—*(Matthew 9:9)*
- Mason—*(2 Kings 12:12)*
- Banker—*(Matthew 25:27)*
- Silversmith—*(Judges 17:4)*
- Potter—*(Jeremiah 18:2)*
- Homemaker—*(Proverbs 31)*

Scene from *Esther: The Girl Who Became Queen*

VeGGie Fun!

• Larry the Cucumber has held some pretty hard and sometimes pretty silly jobs. Can you name some of them and the shows they were in?

I've Been Working on the Railroad . . .

Sheerluck Holmes—The World's Greatest Detective
Lyle the Kindly Viking—A viking
Duke and the Great Pie War— A duke
Minnesota Cuke—An adventurer

Esther: The Girl Who Became Queen—A royal scribe
LarryBoy and the Fib from Outerspace—A superhero

GET TO WORK ON TIME!

Most men and women had very different jobs during Bible times. Here is a look at some of the things that were separated between them:

Men

- Make a living through a trade
- Pay bills and do the trading
- Teach sons their trade
- Teach sons laws and customs
- Find wives for their sons
- Hold political offices
- Plow fields
- Serve as church elders

Women

- Plant crops; collect the food for cooking
- Prepare the meals; grind corn
- Make clothing and blankets; spin and weave thread
- Fetch the water
- Take care of the animals
- Teach daughters how to care for the house
- Help the poor
- Sell garments they have made

Tick Tock, Tick Tock . . .

How did people in the Bible tell time?

It sure wasn't as easy to tell time as it is now. There weren't any watches or clocks.

- Sundials weren't even invented until 1500 BC, which told time using the sun and shadows. This meant you only knew what time it was during the day!

- In 1600 BC water clocks were invented in Egypt. They measured the time by dripping water out of a bucket. Sand clocks, similar to hourglasses, came into being during the Middle Ages.

Veggie Fun!

I'm Still Working on the Railroad

- Can you name some more of Larry the Cucumber's silly jobs and the shows they were in?

Madame Blueberry—A butler
The Ballad of Little Joe—A cowboy, a waiter
Sumo of the Opera—A champion Sumo wrestler
An Easter Carol and *Rack, Shack and Benny*—A factory worker
King George and the Ducky— A king
Going Up—A mover
Jonah–a VeggieTales Movie— A pirate
The Star of Christmas—A playwrite and a star

BIBLE TIME MONEY

For the love of money is a root of all kinds of evil. Some people, eager for money, have wandered from the faith and pierced themselves with many griefs (1 Timothy 6:10).

- **How did people pay for things back in Bible times?** People used to barter or trade for goods and services. People traded things like animals, clothing, food, jewelry, and equipment.

- The first mention of money, or wealth, is in Genesis 13:2.

- A shekel is a unit of weight in silver. One shekel was about a month's wages. Abraham paid Ephron 400 shekels for land to bury his wife *(Genesis 23:16)*.

- A talent was a brick of gold or silver of a certain weight *(Matthew 25)*. A talent was worth 3,000 shekels!

- A denarius was the most current silver coin in the first century of the Christian era. It was a daily wage of a common worker *(Matthew 20:9–10)*, and used to pay the Roman troops. It was also used to pay taxes to Rome.

- A farthing was a small Greek coin that had very little value *(Matthew 10:29)*. A mite was a Hebrew coin that also had very little value *(Mark 12:42)*.

- The Greeks are the first people thought to have created actual coins in the seventh century BC. They were lumps made up of gold, silver, or a mixture of both.

- By AD 1100, gold was the most popular money traded for purchase.

- Because gold was so heavy and difficult to carry, people started issuing promissory notes, the first paper money.

- The Swedes printed the West's first money in 1660. The Chinese had paper money in the 10th Century—300 years before Marco Polo saw it there.

Poverty

- God always takes care of the poor *(Psalms 9:18; 12:5)*.

- God gave Moses specific rules of how to take care of the poor *(Exodus 22:25–27; 23:11; Leviticus 19:9–10; Deuteronomy 24:19–22)*.

- Jesus preached about taking care of the poor *(Matthew 19:21)*. But he also wanted people to be rich in spirit even though they might be poor physically *(Luke 6:20–26)*.

Veggie Bucks

- In the *Stuff-Mart Rap* from the show *Madame Blueberry*, can you name some of the things that the salesmen were trying to sell to Madame Blueberry? Here are a few: A big hat, a tube of glue, 20-gallon Wok, refrigerator, giant air-compressor, dehydrated strudel, nose ring for your poodle, five-pound can of tuna, scuba flippers, a rubber hose, rhododendron tree, wrap-around deck, window scraper, gross of toilet paper, a ratchet set and pliers, solar turkey chopper, gopher bopper, flannel shirt for looking grungy, and a rope for going bungee (come on!).

Did you know . . .

- While the Bible devotes approximately 500 different verses to prayer; about that many verses to faith; it talks about money and possessions in about 1,000 verses!

Veggie Fun!

- In the Silly Song *His Cheeseburger*, what is the discount on bacon and eggs? Half price.

BIBLE TIME MEASUREMENTS

- **What did people use to measure things in Bible times?** During Jesus's time, people used whatever was readily available to take measurements, such as a hand or an arm! For example, a cubit is about 18 inches, the distance from the end of a man's longest finger to his elbow. A span was the width of a man's hand with his fingers spread apart.

Some interesting lengths . . .

- **A man's foot is thought to be how long?** 1 foot, silly!

- **How wide is a man's palm?** About 3 inches. This was called a handbreadth.

- **How long is a man's thumb?** Approximately 1 inch from the tip to the knuckle. A finger was called a digit.

- **How long from a man's nose to his fingertip on an outstretched arm?** About 1 yard.

- **What's a fathom?** 4 cubits or 2 yards.

114

Bible Time Transportation

- God gave us awesome abilities to do amazing things! One of those things has been the development of transportation. Does that go all the way back to Bible times? You bet!

- What was the first type of transportation? Feet! People walked a lot!

- What came after walking? Animals. In 5000 BC, people realized that animals could be harnessed and used for pulling things around, including themselves. Oxen and donkeys were used to carry very heavy loads. Horses were used after oxen and donkeys.

- How did people cross waterways? Rafts, canoes, and rowboats.

It wasn't until 3500 BC that the Egyptians began making their first larger boats.

- When were wheels invented? Around 4,000 BC in Mesopotamia, the first wheels were created out of wood. Wheels were then used to create chariots, carts, and wagons (*Judges 4:2–3*).

VeGGie Fun!

Getting Around Veggie-Style

- Bob the Tomato is driving a van at the beginning of *Jonah–a VeggieTales Movie.* What is the logo that is on the front of the van? VT.

- What do the license plates say on the van? IN A PKL.

- In the VeggieTales show *Esther: The Girl Who Became Queen*, Haman drives around the city in a huge black car which is typical for a gangster. But what is it about the car that is unusual? Instead of wheels, it is carried around by four peas.

LOVE AND MARRIAGE IN BIBLE TIMES

- **How old were girls when they were engaged to be married?** Between the ages of thirteen and seventeen, although their future husbands were usually in their older teens.

- **How did boys and girls fall in love and get married?** Usually, parents made the arrangements and the groom paid a gift to the family before the wedding could happen.

- **How much was a bride worth?** It was customary to pay about fifty shekels for a new bride, although payment could be made through gifts of animals, jewelry, or other items or services. A woman who was widowed or divorced was only worth half that amount.

- **What is a betrothal?** That was a legal arrangement, or promise, made by a man and woman one year prior to getting married.

What Was a Wedding Like in Bible Times?

- The groom and groomsmen would go to the bride's home, without her knowing when, and make a lot of noise to have her come out. Then the marriage ceremony would take place beneath the man's prayer shawl. The fringes on the prayer shawl represent authority and were called wings, meaning that the woman was now under her husband's authority, and he had taken the bride "under his wings" to provide for her. After the wedding they entered into a honeymoon chamber for a few hours as their first time to be alone together. When they came out, the wedding feast was served and all of the people celebrated for seven days.

It's All About Love

- In *The Star of Christmas*, Cavis and Millward (Bob and Larry) set out to teach London the true meaning of Christmas with their play *The Princess and the Plumber*. In the play, who plays the princess? Miss Effie Pickering (Madame Blueberry).

- Cavis and Millward thought they could create a better show about love by "borrowing" the star of Christmas. But when they went about "borrowing" it, they got something else instead. What was it? **The Turtle of Damascus.**

- While in jail, Cavis and Millward meet Charles Pincher. What does he say it would be easier to do than to teach London to love? It would be easier to teach a horse to fly than to teach the city to love.

FESTIVALS, FEASTS, AND TRADITIONS

*For seven days celebrate the Feast to the L*ORD *your God at the place the L*ORD *will choose. For the L*ORD *your God will bless you in all your harvest and in all the work of your hands, and your joy will be complete (Deuteronomy 16:15).*

Bible Feasts:

How many can you name?

- The Feast of Lights or Hanukkah—lasts eight days. This is to celebrate the Jews having enough oil to light the temple candles after the battle of the Maccabees. This is also called the Feast of Dedication *(John 10:22).*

- The Feast of Jubilee—Held every fiftieth year. *(Leviticus 25:8, 10)* Also called the Year of Freedom *(Ezekiel 46:17)* and the Year of the Redemption *(Isaiah 63:4).* The Feast of Jubilee involved a year of release from indebtedness and bondage of all sorts. All prisoners and captives were set free, slaves released, and debtors absolved.

All property reverted to original owners. This plan gave new opportunity to people who had fallen on hard times.

- Year of Feast of the New Moon—celebrated the first day of the month *(Numbers 10:10)* as a memorial to God.

- Feast of Pentecost—held fifty days after Passover *(Leviticus 23:15–16).* Also called Feast of Harvest, Day of First Fruits, Feast of Weeks, and Day of Pentecost. It lasted one day and was a dedication to the first fruits of the harvest.

- Feast of Trumpets—held the first day of the seventh month as an offering to God in connection to Feast of Pentecost *(Leviticus 23:24).*

- **Day of Atonement**—held ten days after Feast of Trumpets as a day to confess sins and make sacrifices.

- **Feast of Purim**—to celebrate the defeat of Haman's wicked plot against the Jews *(Esther 9:24–26)*.

- **Feast of Tabernacles**—began five days after Day of Atonement and lasted eight days. It was to celebrate the Jews being able to enter into the Promised Land after forty years in the wilderness *(Deuteronomy 16:13)*.

- **Feast of the Passover**—This very special feast day in Israel's religious calendar is to remind those of what took place in the Exodus and to mark the day of redemption from Egypt *(Exodus 12: 1–2)*.

- **The Three Annual Feasts**—to honor God *(Exodus 23:14)*.

Veggie Fun!

The Veggie Appetite

- What are the three things that Little Joe serves at the Rootin' Tootin' Pizza Place in Dodgeball City? **Pepperoni Pizza, Root Beer, and Cherry Slushies.**

- In "The Bunny Song" from *Rack, Shack and Benny,* what are some of the foods that Mr. Nezzer and the Asparagus Singers say they don't want? Soup, bread, beans, tofu, pickles, and honey.

- In *The Ballad of Little Joe,* during the years of famine, Little Joe's brothers have to share one very small meal with one another. What is it? One pancake.

MORE FESTIVALS, FEASTS AND TRADITIONS

Passover

- **What is Passover?** A Jewish celebration that honors the flight from captivity in Egypt *(Exodus 12:1–20)*.

- **When does Passover take place, and how long does it last?** Late March or early April, and it lasts for one week *(Leviticus 23:4–8)*.

- **What special foods are to be eaten and why? Roasted lamb** to represent the lamb's blood that was sacrificed and put on the doors so that the angel of death would pass over; **unleavened bread** to show that the Israelites were in a hurry to leave and had no time to make bread with yeast; and **bitter herbs** to remind them of their time during slavery *(Exodus 12)*.

St. Patrick's Day

How much do you know about this special day?

- St. Patrick, whose real name was Maewyn Succat, was a missionary who helped to convert the Irish to Christianity in the AD 400s. (But he wasn't Irish himself!)

- St. Patrick used a shamrock, which looks like a three-leaf clover, as a metaphor to explain the Father, Son, and Holy Spirit (the Trinity).

- People wear green because it symbolizes the season of spring, along with the shamrock.

Be My Valentine

How much do you know about this day of love?

- Dr. Valentine was a priest and physician who lived in Rome during the third century.

- Dr. Valentine was imprisoned and killed because he was a Christian who was not willing to deny his faith.

- The Romans wanted young men to go to war, so they decreed that they were not to marry. Dr. Valentine, however, married them in secret—and so began his connection with this holiday of love!

Endangered Love

The Veggies had some silly fun with some love songs . . .

- In the Silly Song "Endangered Love," who is "the one for me" that Larry sings about? **Barbara Manatee.**

- In *Love Songs with Mr. Lunt*, Mr. Lunt sings about his love for what fast food? His cheeseburger.

- In the Silly Song, "Sport Utility Vehicle," who does Larry run into at the gas station? Miss Akmetha.

- In Larry's classic Silly Song, "Love My Lips," who would Larry call if his lips moved to Duluth, left a mess, and took his tooth? His dad.

THE ARTS

There is a time for everything, and a season for every activity under heaven (Ecclesiastes 3:1).

Theater/Drama

- The Israelites had no drama or theaters. However, we know that the Greeks and Romans had theaters for dramatic presentations and public gatherings. Acts 19:29–31 mentions a theater in Ephesus where Paul had trouble talking to people who didn't want to quit worshiping the goddess Artemis. This theater sat about 25,000 people.

- The very first dramas were written by the ancient Greeks to please their gods. They performed these dramas at festivals and celebrations. The actors would often wear masks to show the part they were playing. Actors in a chorus would perform songs and dances to explain the story taking place on the stage.

Music and Instruments

- **What were the very first instruments in the Bible?** The harp and flute. They were first played by Jubal, who was the great-great-grandson of Cain *(Genesis 4:21).*

- How many other instruments can you name that appeared in the Bible?

  Flute *(Psalm 150:4; Luke 7:32)*
  Gong *(1 Corinthians 13:2)*
  Harp *(Psalm 150:3; Revelation 5:8)*
  Horn *(Joshua 6:4; Psalm 81:3)*
  Bell *(Exodus 28:33–35)*
  Sistrum or musical rattle *(2 Samuel 6:5)*
  Organ *(Job 21:12)*
  Lyre or hand-held harp *(Psalm 43:4; Isaiah 5:12)*
  Trumpet *(Numbers 10:8–10)*
  Tambourine *(Exodus 15:20; Psalm 68:25)*
  Shofar, a ram's horn *(Joshua 6:20)*
  Timbrel, a form of tambourine *(Job 21:12)*
  Cymbal *(1 Chronicles 15:16; Psalm 150:5)*

- Small harps and flutes are mentioned early in the Old Testament, and possibly were instruments that were taken on the ark with Noah and his family.

- In 2000 BC (when Jacob and Esau lived), the first trumpets were being played in what we now know as Denmark.

- By the time Joseph was in Pharaoh's house, percussion instruments, like drums, were being used in Egyptian music.

Dance

Dancing was first mentioned in Exodus 15:19–21.
- Celebration dancing—*1 Samuel 18:6–7*
- Dancing before the Lord— *2 Samuel 6:14–16*
- Sorrow turned into dancing— *Psalm 30:11*
- Dances of praise—*Psalms 149:3; 150:4*

Art

- Cave paintings are among the oldest forms of art. People used tools made from stone called flint to paint pictures of the things they did.

- Mosaics were created out of glass and stone. These Mosaics were used for various different things like hanging artwork, wall decorations, table tops, and flooring.

- Special jewelry was created as an art form. Women created hairpieces, brooches, pins, earrings, necklaces, and bracelets.

Veggie-tainment

- In the "Bunny Song" from *Rack, Shack and Benny*, what vegetables sing back-up for Mr. Nezzer? The Asparagus Girls.

- At the beginning of the "VeggieTales Theme Song," why does Larry the Cucumber say he can't play the guitar? Because he doesn't have any hands.

- In what Silly Song does Larry the Cucumber play the accordion? *School House Polka!*

SPORTS, GAMES, AND TOYS

What types of toys were played with during Bible times?

- In Egypt, clay balls were probably the first toys. Joseph's sons may have played with them as children.

- After the invention of the wheel in Mesopotamia in 3500 BC, small figurines like horses and wheels were pulled by kids—similar to what children play with today.

- Ancient Greek children played with rattles, whistles, yo-yos, pull toys, clay animals, and terracotta dolls.

Batter Up!

What sporting events took place during Bible times?

- Athletic games were held to honor false gods, and some were held as offerings of thanksgiving to them. They were both a social and religious event.

- The very first gymnasts began in Crete, between the time of the Old and New Testaments. The player would run toward a charging bull, grab its horns, and when tossed into the air, land on the bull's back, then flip off the back onto the ground!

- Greece held athletic games with parades, feasts, and music. Once professional athletes began to play, however, there were fewer and fewer participants. The Greeks seemed to enjoy playing more than watching their sporting events!

- In Rome, things were different. People only watched the games played by slaves, prisoners, or professionals. At times, games were staged between the prisoners until someone died.

- Ever hear of a gladiator? These professional fighters or slaves trained for battle with each other or wild animals during New Testament times.

- Other New Testament games were foot races, wrestling, training for contests, and competing.

- The very first Olympic Games were held in Olympia, Greece, in 776 BC.

Toys and Games

- In the show *Madame Blueberry,* what toy does Junior ask his dad for while they are in the Stuff-Mart? The Casey Junior Deluxe Train Set (with working lights and real livestock smell!).

- What toy does he get instead? A big red bouncy ball.

- In the movie *Jonah—a VeggieTales Movie,* what two games do The Pirates Who Don't Do Anything play with Jonah on the deck of the ship? Ping pong and Go Fish®.

- In the show *LarryBoy and the Fib from Outer Space,* who does Junior's dad say is the greatest bowler who ever rolled a ball? Art Bigotti.

- Name at least five types of sporting equipment that could be found on the Pirates' ship. Here are a few to get you started: surfboard, croquet mallets, bowling ball, lawn darts, badminton racquet, boxing gloves, soccer ball, ping-pong table, ping-pong paddles, ping-pong balls, hopscotch board, dart board, basketball hoop.

INTERESTING STUFF
IN INTERESTING PLACES

What was Rome like during the apostle Paul's lifetime?

- It was built on seven low, flat hills.
- The population was 1 million, and it was one of the biggest cities in the world.
- The Roman Empire ruled most of the land around the Mediterranean Sea.
- Prices were very high. People were either very rich or very poor.
- Rich people had homes with swimming pools and gardens.
- There were apartments that housed several families.
- Homes had sewers, but there were no streetlights at night.
- Water was carried into the city by aqueducts, similar to our plumbing system now.
- The city also had libraries, bookstores, and even sports arenas. The Romans also enjoyed watching chariot races, fighting gladiators, and going to public baths to relax, get clean, and exercise.

- It wasn't until AD 392 that the Roman emperor Theodosus made Christianity the state religion of the Roman Empire.

What was Egypt like during Bible times?

- The Egyptians started out as farmers who lived along the banks of the Nile River.
- Egyptian writing was made up of over 700 pictures and symbols called hieroglyphs.
- Their kings were called pharaohs and when they died they were buried inside the huge stone pyramids built on the edge of the deserts.
- The Egyptians tried to preserve the dead, thinking that would provide them with another life after they died. So they took out their insides, dried out the body, wrapped it in cloths, and put them into a coffin. They were called mummies.

How much do you know about Greece many years ago?

Veggie Fun!

The Veggies Went to Town

- It was much different than the Greece we know today. Each city had its own ruler.
- The greatest city was Athens, which was known for its wisdom, knowledge, and theater.
- Huge buildings made of stone were built to honor their gods and goddesses.
- The Greeks strongly believed that performance arts would honor their gods. So during festivals, a great deal of theater took place, with prizes being awarded for the best.
- The people in Greece were highly competitive, so they organized games and athletics. In fact, the Olympics originated in Olympia, Greece.

- In the show *The Toy That Saved Christmas*, what was the name of the town that didn't "get" Christmas? Dinkletown.

- Mr. Nezzer's toy factory is in Dinkletown, but his delivery penguins are unable to deliver to a neighboring town. What town is it? Puggslyville. Why are they unable to deliver there? The Puggslyville Bridge has collapsed.

- In the show *Jonah–a VeggieTales Movie*, Angus, the cruise ticket salesman, tells Jonah that he can't sail to Nineveh. Why? Because it's land locked.

- Where does Angus suggest Jonah go to get as far away from Nineveh as he can? He tells him to sail down to Egypt. (It's lovely this time of year.)

- What two kingdoms were at war with each other in *Duke and the Great Pie War*? The kingdoms of Rhubarb and Scone.

POPULAR PLACES

The world population has exploded since Bible times! In AD 1 the world population was 300 million. Today, there are approximately 6.4 billion people. By 2050, scientists feel it will grow to 9 billion!

• **Most sparsely populated country?** Mongolia with 4.7 people per square mile.

• **Most densely populated country?** Monaco with 43,045 people per square mile.

• **Most densely populated state in the United States?** New Jersey with 1,130 people per square mile.

1.	Jerusalem	767	times
2.	Egypt	558	times
3.	Heaven	551	times
4.	Babylon	260	times
5.	Jordan	179	times
6.	Samaria	115	times
7.	Canaan	88	times
8.	Galilee	71	times
9.	Bethlehem	38	times
10.	Sinai	36	times

Facts about different places . . .

• Mount Ararat where Noah's ark came to rest is the tallest Bible mountain—approximately 16,900 feet above sea level.

• Shortest Bible mountain is the mountain of Jesus's temptation—1,148 feet above sea level.

• Mount Moriah is the place where Abraham went to sacrifice his son Isaac; it is now occupied by the Dome of the Rock in Jerusalem.

• Oldest city—on the site of Jericho was found a stone tower that is at least 7,000 years old. Possibly built before the pyramids.

• The city of Nineveh had more than 120,000 people and took three full days to walk around it *(Jonah 3:3)*.

How many times do these places appear in the Bible? ◄

The Sea of Galilee

- How big is the Sea of Galilee? Twelve miles long and seven miles wide.

- Where is the Sea of Galilee? North of the Dead Sea. The Jordan River flows through the Sea of Galilee and into the Dead Sea.

- What happened at the Sea of Galilee? Jesus sat in a boat while on this sea and preached to people on the shore *(Matthew 13:2–3)*, and Jesus also walked on the Sea of Galilee *(Matthew 14:22–33)*. This sea is also known for having many fish and for its strong storms.

- What are some other names for the Sea of Galilee? The Sea of Galilee is also known as the Sea of Tiberius *(John 6:1)* or the Lake of Gennesaret *(Luke 5:1)*.

Veggie Fun!

In All Our Veggie Voyages!

- Minnesota Cuke believed a rogue band of Canadian barrel makers were in search of Samson's Hairbrush in order to gain control of what natural landmark? They wanted to gain control of both sides of Niagara Falls.

- The Snoodles live in Snoodleburg. What land is Snoodleburg in? The Land of Galoots.

- In the countertop scene for the show *Snoodle's Tale*, Bob thinks Larry has been away at camp. What is the name of the camp? Danish Immersion Camp.

BIBLE TIME BUILDINGS
A Bible Time House

Where did people live in Bible times?

- The Israelites initially lived in tents *(Genesis 47:3)* as they were, by occupation, shepherds. However, the first buildings recorded in the Bible were in *Genesis 10:11–12* and *11:4, 8.*

- In Jericho, the oldest city in the world, houses were initially built of mud bricks. These were made by hand and left to dry in the sun *(Genesis 11:3)*. Later, straw was added to the mud, which made the bricks much stronger.

- Originally all houses were round. However, as neighborhoods were formed, houses were made rectangular in shape like they are today.

- Homes didn't have the luxury of the bathrooms we enjoy today. Most people bathed in rivers until the time of the Judges. That's when showers were invented in Egypt and Greece. The first toilet and sewer system was developed in Mesopotamia.

- Larger homes were built with a courtyard enclosed. *(2 Samuel 17:18; Nehemiah 8:16).* The homes had flat roofs and a low wall so the roof could be used for other living purposes. Steps were built up to the roof from the outside of the house *(Luke 5:19).*

- Some homes had an additional upper room that was used as a private chamber, bedroom, or apartment for guests. *(2 Samuel 18:33; 2 Kings 4:8–10; 23:12; Daniel 6:10).*

(cont. to page 132)

Oh, the Places Veggies Go

- In *Sheerluck Holmes*, what is the name of the pub where Sheerluck and Watson hang out with their friends? Doylies.

- Sheerluck and his trusty sidekick, Watson, are called on to solve a robbery. Where did the robbery take place? Buckingham Palace.

MORE ABOUT BIBLE TIME BUILDINGS

(cont. from page 130)

• The poor often rented rooms in apartments. Wealthier people had large, comfortable homes with running water and furnaces. The first water system to bring water into a city was built by the Assyrians in 691 BC. It brought water into Nineveh. Some windows opened into the courtyard and were covered by a lattice *(Judges 5:28)*. The furniture in homes consisted of couches, pillows, chairs, tables, lanterns, or lamps. *(2 Kings 4:10; Amos 6:4; Matthew 5:15)*.

How did the wealthy Romans heat their homes and baths?

• When Jesus was a child, the Roman homes and baths used the Hypocaust System for heating the building and the pools. Passageways under the floor carried hot air heated from basement fires to the floors above. In some baths the floors would be so hot that the bathers would have to wear wooden sandals to keep their feet from being burned. The fires in the basement were kept going by slaves.

What kind of tools were used for building in Bible times?

• The tools utilized in building included the plumb line *(Amos 7:7)*; the measuring reed *(Ezekiel 40:3)*; and the saw *(1 Kings 7:9)*.

A Bit About Spiritual Buildings . . .

- Jesus called Peter a rock, then said, "On this rock I will build my church" *(Matthew 16:18).*

- All believers are considered "God's building" *(1 Corinthians 3:9).*

- Heaven is called "a building from God" *(2 Corinthians 5:1).*

- Christ is the only real foundation of the church *(1 Corinthians 3:10–12).*

Mr. Nezzer's Plastic Egg Factory

Veggie Fun!

Very Veggie Buildings

- What is the name of the restaurant that Mr. Lunt sings about in his song "His Cheeseburger"? Burger Bell.

- Mr. Nezzer has owned three different factories in three different VeggieTales shows. Can you name the factories and the shows they were in? The Chocolate Factory in *Rack, Shack and Benny*; The Toy Factory in *The Toy That Saved Christmas*; and the Plastic Egg Factory in *An Easter Carol.*

PLACES TO WORSHIP
The Tabernacle

- **What is the tabernacle?** A special tent God instructed the Israelites to build to worship him *(Exodus 25–30; 35–40)*. This tent could be carried wherever the Israelites went.

In Exodus 25 and 26, God gave specifications for building the tabernacle:

- **How big was it?** 45 feet long, 15 feet wide, and 15 feet high. Around the tent was a wall 150 feet long on two sides and 75 feet long on the other two sides.

- **What was inside the tent?** Special objects that God instructed to be placed there. Only one doorway went through the outer wall into the Holy Tent. The Holy Tent was divided into two rooms. The first room was 30 feet long and the second room was 15 feet long. The second room was the Most Holy Place, where the ark of the covenant was placed.

- **What did the ark of the covenant look like?** It was covered in gold and had two gold creatures with wings on the top.

- Once a year, on the Day of Atonement, the high priest went into the Most Holy Place and sprinkled blood of a sacrifice on the top of it. A priest had to go through purification rites to cleanse himself prior to entering the Most Holy Place *(Numbers 19)*. The priest carried incense burning in front of him to have smoke between himself and God's presence. He wore a blue ephod (a long vest) with bells on it *(Exodus 28:31–35)* so that the others knew he was alive while inside.

The town square clock tower from *A Snoodle's Tale*

More Veggie Buildings

- Right in the heart of Snoodleburg stood a curious building (the tallest around). What was it? A clock tower where Snoodles were created.

- In the show *Duke and the Great Pie War*, what kind of a building do Petunia and Nona live in when Duke Duke meets them? A tree stump.

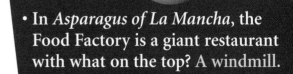

- In *Asparagus of La Mancha*, the Food Factory is a giant restaurant with what on the top? A windmill.

135

THE TEMPLE

> *The temple is first used in relation to the tabernacle, and it was called "the temple of the LORD" (1 Samuel 3:3).*

The temple was also called:

- the holy temple *(Psalm 79:1)*
- the house of the Lord
  (2 Chronicles 23:5, 12)
- the house of the God of Jacob
  (Isaiah 2:3)
- the house of my glory
  (Isaiah 60:7)
- the house of prayer *(Isaiah 56:7)*
- the house of sacrifice
  (2 Chronicles 7:12)
- the holy mount *(Isaiah 27:13)*
- the mount of the Lord's house
  (Isaiah 2:2)
- the palace for the Lord God
  (1 Chronicles 29:1)
- Zion *(Psalms 74:2; 84:7)*
- my [Jesus's] Father's house
  (John 2:16)

In the New Testament, the word *temple* is used in even more ways:
- It is figuratively used as Christ's human body *(John 2:19, 21)*.
- Believers are called "God's temple" *(1 Corinthians 3:16–17)*.
- The church is designated "a holy temple in the Lord" *(Ephesians 2:21)*.
- Heaven also has a temple. *(Revelation 15:5)*.

- What was the temple like? God gave exact instructions on how to build the temple *(1 Kings 5–8)*. God told the Jewish people to build the temple in Jerusalem patterned after the tabernacle.

- How was the temple built? King Solomon had the temple built to be about 30 feet wide, 87 feet long, and 43 feet high. It was built of stone and elaborately decorated with special woods, carvings, and metals. The inner room (the Most Holy Place) held the ark of the covenant. The main room had decorations and gold everywhere. At the front of the temple was a porch with large pillars. In the courtyard of the temple was an altar for burning offerings. The temple of God had so much bronze in it that it couldn't be weighed (*2 Kings 25:16*).

- What was the temple used for? It was a house for God, and only the priests could go in.

- How long did it take to build the temple? Seven years.

- How long did the temple last? Approximately 374 years until it was destroyed.

- Was the temple ever rebuilt? Yes, the foundation of the second temple was laid in 535 BC and finally finished on March 12, 515 BC. This temple was enlarged by King Herod and stood for 585 years, before being destroyed in AD 70 when Titus, a Roman general, invaded Jerusalem.

Madame Blueberry's treehouse

Veggie Fun!

And Even More Veggie Buildings

- Besides having a LOT of stuff in it, what is unusual about Madame Blueberry's house? It's built in a tree.

- In the show, *The Star of Christmas*, what happens to the theater that Cavis and Millward have their show in? It burns down.

137

ARCHAEOLOGICAL FINDS IN THE BIBLE

Did you know . . .

For a long time the Bible was believed to be the only book that contained historical information about the past. Since that time, archaeologists have uncovered lots of information to prove that there were other books with similar information. They have also made discoveries to prove that what the Bible says is true!

- So what is archaeology? It's the study of past human cultures. People who study archaeology are called archaeologists.

- **How do archaeologists figure out stuff like that?** They study writings on the walls—some *actual* walls, and some in caves, mountains, cliffs, and so on. They also uncover pottery, clay writing tablets, skeletons, weapons, rocks, and even parts of entire buildings that may have been buried and had things built upon them!

- In 1947, a shepherd boy went exploring in a cave by the Dead Sea hoping to find gold. Instead he found some very old clay pots that held Old Testament scrolls. This helped prove that the Old Testament we have today hasn't changed since it was first written.

- In June 1880, a boy fell into the Pool of Siloam and saw a small hole. He explored and discovered King Hezekiah's secret tunnel that was built about 700 years before Jesus was born. The tunnel was used to link the people of Jerusalem to their only water source when enemies surrounded them *(2 Chronicles 32:30)*.

- The Tablets of Gilgamesh are twelve stone tablets that were found in the Babylon area (near modern day Iraq) and may be the oldest written story unearthed to date. *The Epic of Gilgamesh* dates to about 2700 BC and was originally written on twelve clay tablets. The eleventh tablet contains an extensive flood story similar to the biblical account in Genesis. They help prove that there really was a flood that covered the earth.

Dinosaurs in the Bible?

Are dinosaurs in the Bible? No one knows for sure. But there are two animals described in the Bible that sound pretty interesting:

- In *Job 40:15–24*, an animal is described as one who eats grass, is very strong, and has a tail like a cedar tree, the behemoth. Some people believe that this might be referring to a Brachiosaur, the largest dinosaur, because verse 19 says that the behemoth "ranks first among the works of God" or is the largest animal God made.

- In Job 41, Psalm 104:25–26, and Isaiah 27:1, Leviathan is an animal described as a large whale-like sea animal with fearsome teeth and fire coming out of his mouth *(Job 41:19–21)*.

- In 1676 the very first dinosaur fossil was found in England.

- In 1990 a 90 percent complete T-Rex skeleton was found in South Dakota. Dinosaur fossils have been found in every one of the United States, in addition to Canada, Mexico, South America, Africa, Asia, Europe, Antarctica, and Australia.

Can you find . . .

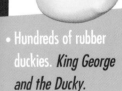

Through the years there have been all kinds of interesting "finds" in VeggieTales shows. Can you name the shows in which the following interesting artifacts can be found?

- A wind-up blue lobster. *The Story of Flibber-o-loo.*
- A rocket car. *The Star of Christmas.*

- An Art Bigotti bowling plate. *LarryBoy and the Fib from Outer Space.*
- Larry's hairbrush. *The Hairbrush Song.*
- The Turtle of Damascus. *The Star of Christmas.*
- The Tiger Bike. *Sumo of the Opera.*

- A huge sombrero. *Dance of the Cucumber.*
- A high silk hat. *Larry's High Silk Hat.*
- A flying milk truck. *Rack, Shack and Benny.*
- A stuffed manatee named Barbara. *Endangered Love.*

- Hundreds of rubber duckies. *King George and the Ducky.*
- A bubble pipe. *Sheerluck Holmes and the Golden Ruler.*
- Samson's hairbrush. *Minnesota Cuke and the Search for Samson's Hairbrush.*

MIRACLES

You are the God who performs miracles;
you display your power among the peoples (Psalm 77:14).

Jesus and New Testament Miracles

• What is the Latin meaning of the word *miracle*? It means "wonderful thing."

Jesus's miracles were done to show that he was, indeed, God's Son. Jesus said, "*I and the Father are one*" *(John 10:30).*

• After Jesus performed the miracle of healing ten men who had leprosy, how many came back to thank him? Just one.

• Jesus performed four different types of miracles. What were they? **Miracles of Nature**—He stopped a storm on the sea and walked on water. **Miracles of Healing**—He healed many from their illnesses. **Miracles over Evil Spirits**—He commanded demons out. **Miracles over Death**—He raised Lazarus and the daughter of Jairus from death. Most of all, Jesus himself arose from death!

• What was Jesus's biggest miracle? His resurrection!

• Whom did the angels rescue from jail? Peter *(Acts 12:5–11).*

• Who persecuted Jesus's followers, was blinded by a great light, and became one of Jesus's greatest preachers? Saul, who later became known as Paul *(Acts 9:1–6).*

• What's the only miracle performed by Jesus recorded in all four Gospels? The feeding of the 5,000.

• How did Paul and Silas get out of prison? God caused an earthquake that opened the bars, but they did not escape. Instead, they stayed and converted the prison master to Christianity *(Acts 16:25–34).*

- What happened when a poison-ous snake bit Paul in Malta? Paul shook off the snake and was not harmed (*Acts 28:3–6*).

- What are the four Greek words used to designate miracles in the New Testament?
  1. sign (*Matthew 12:38*)
  2. wonder (*Acts 2:19*)
  3. miracle (*Acts 2:22*)
  4. works (*John 5:20* KJV).

Get Me to the Church on Time

- There is only one vehicle that can get Cavis and Millward to the church in time to save the Christmas pageant. What vehicle do they take? Seymour's Rocket Carriage.

- Seymour (Pa Grape) gives them one strict instruction before they take off in the Rocket Carriage. What is it? Under no circum-stances are they to use rocket number eleven. Why? Because it hasn't been tested.

- What's the other instruction that Seymour gives them? The brakes only work when the carriage is on the ground. (So try to stay on the ground.)

- On their journey to the church, how many buildings do they hit? Four: the hat wagon, the bakery, the bank, and the church.

There goes the Rocket Carriage!

HOW MANY OF JESUS'S MIRACLES CAN YOU NAME?

- He turned water into wine (*John 2:1–11*).
- He caused a large catch of fish (*Luke 5:1–11*).
- He calmed a storm (*Matthew 8:23–27; Mark 4:35–41; Luke 8:22–25*).
- He fed a hungry crowd of 5,000 with 5 small loaves of bread and 2 fish (*Matthew 14:15–21; Mark 6:35–44; Luke 9:12–17; John 6:5–13*).
- He walked on water (*Matthew 14:22–33; Mark 6:48–51; John 6:19–21*).
- He fed over 4,000 people (*Matthew 15:32–38; Mark 8:1–9*).
- He predicted a coin would be in a fish's mouth (*Matthew 17:24–27*).
- He commanded a fig tree to die (*Matthew 21:18–22; Mark 11:12–14*).
- He healed a man's son in Galilee (*John 4:46–54*).
- He healed Peter's mother–in–law (*Matthew 8:14–15; Mark 1:30–31; Luke 4:38–39*).
- He healed a paralyzed man (*Matthew 9:1–8; Mark 2:1–12; Luke 5:18–25*).
- He healed a leper (*Matthew 8:1–4; Mark 1:40–42; Luke 5:12–13*).
- He healed a man's hand (*Matthew 12:9–13; Mark 3:1–5; Luke 6:6–10*).
- He healed a centurion's servant (*Matthew 8:5–13; Luke 7:1–10*).
- He healed a woman's bleeding (*Matthew 9:20–22; Mark 5:25–29; Luke 8:43–48*).
- Jesus healed two blind men and a mute man (*Matthew 9:27–33*).
- He healed a woman's daughter (*Matthew 15:21–28; Mark 7:24–30*).
- He healed a man who couldn't hear or speak (*Mark 7:31–37*).
- He healed a blind man (*Mark 8:22–26*).
- He healed a child (*Matthew 17:14–21; Mark 9:17–29; Luke 9:38–43*).
- He healed ten lepers (*Luke 17:11–19*).
- He healed a man born blind (*John 9:1–12*).
- He healed a man in a Pharisee's house (*Luke 14:1–6*).
- He healed Malchus's ear (*Luke 22:49–51; John 18:10*).
- He cast out a demon (*Mark 1:23–26; Luke 4:33–35*).

- He healed a demon-possessed man *(Matthew 12:22–37; Luke 11:14)*.
- He cast the devil out of two men *(Matthew 8:28–34; Mark 5:1–15; Luke 8:27–35)*.
- He cast out a demon *(Matthew 9:32–33)*

- He raised a woman's son. *(Luke 7:11–15)*.
- He raised Jairus's daughter *(Matthew 9:18–26; Mark 5:22–24; Luke 8:41–42)*.
- He raised Lazarus *(Luke 11:1–46)*.
- The transfiguration *(Matthew 17:1–8)*.
- The resurrection *(John 21:1–14)*.

And the Walls Came Tumbling Down

- In the VeggieTales show, *Josh and the Big Wall*, how many days did the Israelites have to march around the walls of Jericho before they fell? Seven.

- On the seventh day, how many times did they march around the walls? Seven.

- What kind of vehicle did the peas of Jericho use to pump slushie down on the Israelites as they walked around the wall? A cement truck. Did it stop the Israelites? No.

- What song did the priests play on their horns to cause the walls to fall down? "When the Saints Go Marching In."

- After the walls fell, which VeggieTales character got a piece of dust in his eye and announced, "Boy, did I pick a bad day to wear my contacts?" Jimmy Gourd.

AMAZING BIBLE MIRACLES!

• **What was one of the first amazing shows of God's power that involved a man named Noah?** The flood *(Genesis 7–8)*.

• **How did God speak to Moses?** Through a burning bush *(Exodus 3:3)*.

• **How did God reveal his amazing power through Moses to help him lead the Israelites out of slavery from Egypt?** Through ten plagues:

1. Plague of Blood *(Exodus 7:14–24)*.
2. Plague of Frogs *(Exodus 8:1–15)*.
3. Plague of Gnats *(Exodus 8:16–19)*.
4. Plague of Flies *(Exodus 8:20–32)*.
5. Plague of Livestock *(Exodus 9:1–7)*.
6. Plague of Boils *(Exodus 9:8–12)*.
7. Plague of Hail *(Exodus 9:13–35)*.
8. Plague of Locusts *(Exodus 10:1–20)*.
9. Plague of Darkness *(Exodus 10:21–29)*.
10. Plague of Death for Firstborn *(Exodus 11:1–12:30)*.

• **How did God help Moses when the Egyptians had trapped the Israelites in front of the Red Sea?** By parting the Red Sea, allowing them to cross on dry land *(Exodus 14:21–28)*.

• **What walls did God help Joshua to take down by marching around them?** The walls of Jericho *(Joshua 6:6–20)*.

The Fib was little . . . at first!

- Who received water from a rock? Moses (*Exodus 17:1–6*).

- To whom did God give amazing strength? Samson (*Judges 14–16*).

- Who did the ravens supply food for? Elijah (*1 Kings 17:1–5*).

- Whose leprosy was healed in the Old Testament? Miriam (*Numbers 12*) and Naaman (*2 Kings 5:1–14*).

In the Nick of Time

- By the end of the show, *LarryBoy and the Fib from Outer Space*, the Fib has grown to be so big he is almost as tall as the tallest building in Bumblyburg. What does the giant Fib say to Junior as he is picking him up and carrying him away? "Don't worry, Junior. A little fib couldn't hurt anybody."

- Who finally stops the Fib from Outer Space? Junior Asparagus.

- How does he do it? He tells the truth about breaking his father's collectible Art Bigotti Bowling Plate.

MORE AMAZING BIBLE MIRACLES!

• How did Elisha battle an incoming army? He asked God that they be blinded *(2 Kings 6:18–20)*.

• Who were the three men delivered from a fiery furnace? Shadrach, Meshach, and Abednego *(Daniel 3:10–27)*.

• Who was saved from a den of lions? Daniel *(Daniel 6:16–23)*.

• What prophet was swallowed by a big fish and survived in its belly for three days before being spit back out again onto dry land? Jonah *(Jonah 2:1–10)*.

• How did a widow and her son survive when they no longer had any food? Elijah told her to make him a loaf of bread from a small bit of flour she had left. He also said her jar of flour and jug of oil would not run dry *(1 Kings 17:13–16)*.

• Who stretched himself over a dead boy and brought him back to life? Elijah, through a miracle from God *(1 Kings 17:17–23)*.

• What type of miracles did Jesus do? Jesus's miracles can be put into four different categories: miracles of nature, miracles of healing, miracles over death, and miracles over evil spirits.

• Who parted the Jordan River, using his rolled-up cloak? Elijah, through a miracle from God *(2 Kings 2:13–14)*.

- Were any miracles performed through the apostles? Yes, God performed several miracles through the apostles. Peter healed a lame man *(Acts 3:1–8)* and he raised a woman from death *(Acts 9:32–40)*. Philip performed miracles *(Acts 8:6–7)*; Paul caused an evil man to be blind for a while *(Acts 13:6–11)*, made a lame man walk *(Acts 14:8–10)*, cast out demons *(Acts 16:16–18)*, and did many other miracles to help people believe in Jesus. Barnabas also did miracles when he was with Paul *(Acts 14:3)*.

The Truth Be Told!

- At the end of *LarryBoy and the Rumor Weed*, the Rumor Weed is huge and she is going to hurt Alfred. What is the rumor that has caused her to grow so big? Alfred is a dangerous robot with laser eyes (who's going to take over the world).

Veggie Fun!

- What Veggie characters started the rumor about Alfred? Junior Asparagus and Laura Carrot.

- How did they stop the Rumor Weed? By spreading nice words instead of words that can hurt.

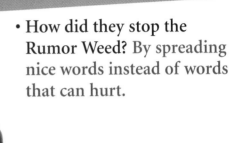

147

ANGELS

What is an angel?

The word *angel* means "messenger." They are invisible spirits, although God has allowed a few select people to see them. They are powerful *(2 Thessalonians 1:7)*, but they are not as powerful as God.

How many things can you name that angels do?

- They disguise themselves as ordinary people *(Genesis 18:1–2; 19:1)*.
- They lead God's people *(Exodus 23:20–21)*.
- They explain God's plans *(Daniel 10:13–14)*.
- They watch over us *(Psalm 34:7; Matthew 18:10)*.
- They praise God *(Isaiah 6:1–4)*.
- They deliver God's messages *(Matthew 1:20)*.
- They help God's people *(Psalm 91:11)*.
- They hear our prayers *(Luke 1:13)*.
- They rejoice over people who turn to God instead of sin *(Luke 15:7, 10)*.
- They punish God's enemies *(Acts 12:21–23)*.

What Else Do You Know about Angels?

- How many angels are mentioned by name in the Bible? Three. Who are they? Gabriel *(Daniel 8:16; Luke 1:19, 26)*, Michael *(Jude 1:9)*, and Lucifer *(Isaiah 14:12 KJV)*.

- How many angels are there? According to the Bible, there are tens of thousands! *(Daniel 7:10)*.

- How many times did angels appear to or help people in the Bible? 233.

- Who created angels, and how long do they live? God created them, and they will never pass away *(Psalm 148)*.

What are angels like?

- They were created holy *(Mark 8:38)*.
- They are intelligent *(Matthew 28:5; 1 Peter 1:12)*.
- Angels have emotions *(Job 38:7; Luke 2:13)*.
- Angels make decisions *(Jude 6)*.
- Angels can only be in one place at one time *(Daniel 9:21–23; 10:10–14)*.
- Angels cannot have children *(Mark 12:25)*.
- Angels do not die *(Luke 20:36)*.
- Angels have more knowledge than man *(Matthew 24:31)* but less than God *(Matthew 24:36)*.
- Angels have more power than man but less than God *(2 Peter 2:11; Acts 5:19)*.

- Do you have to see angels for them to be present? No! *(Hebrews 13:2)*.

- Can angels speak different languages? Yes, many *(1 Corinthians 13:1–2)*.

- Are all angels good? Unfortunately not! They may have been created holy *(Mark 8:38)*, but some angels turned against God and are under Satan's leadership. These angels are referred to as demons *(Matthew 25:41; Ephesians 6:12; 2 Peter 2:4; Jude 6)*.

Veggie-Angels

- What *Silly Song with Larry* features three peas dressed as angels and carrying slices of pizza? "Pizza Angel."

- In the show *An Easter Carol*, a music box angel named Hope takes Ebenezer Nezzer on a wild tour through his life in the past, present, and future. When they go to Easter future, what happens to the stained-glass window in the church? A wrecking ball breaks through it!

AMAZING DISCOVERIES FROM THE BIBLE

Whatever wisdom may be, it is far off and most profound—who can discover it? (Ecclesiastes 7:24).

Advances and Inventions

The **earliest** devices:

- A sickle was used for cutting crops—*Deuteronomy 16:9*
- People stored things in animal skins—*1 Samuel 25:18*
- Bricks were made from mud—*Genesis 11:13*

The **first** music:

- The harp and organ—*Genesis 4:2* KJV
- Tambourines—*Genesis 31:27*
- Songs—*Exodus 15:1–18*
- Trumpets—*Numbers 10:10*
- Music ministry—*1 Chronicles 6:32*
- Choir singers—*Nehemiah 12:47*

Discoveries in the Bible:

- No actual "moonlight"—*Job 25:5* KJV
- Light travels—*Job 38:19*
- Stars cannot be counted—*Genesis 15:5; 22:17*
- Cosmic light—*Genesis 1:3; Psalm 74:16*
- Empty place in the north—*Job 26:7*
- Earth is suspended in space—*Job 26:7*
- Sound waves from stars—*Job 38:7*
- Pleiades star cluster and Orion's belt—*Job 38:31*
- Earth is not flat—*Isaiah 40:22*
- Sea springs—*Job 38:16; Proverbs 8:28*
- Sea canyons—*2 Samuel 22:16*
  - Ocean currents—*Psalm 8:8*
    - Running water is more sanitary—*Leviticus 15:13* KJV

Very Veggie Inventions?

- Where did Qwerty the computer get its name? Qwerty is named after the first six letters on the U.S. English keyboard: the letters proceed from left to right: Q-W-E-R-T-Y.

He who is greedy for gain troubles his own house....
Proverbs 15:27

- The Astonishing Contraption of Silliness is featured in what show? *The Ultimate Silly Song Countdown.*

- The show *Auto-Tainment* features a crazy contraption that, according to Larry, can generate the entertainment of the future. What are the two mechanical components of the contraption? The Wheel of Veggies and the Swarming Balls of Disorder.

- In the show *God Wants Me to Forgive Them!?!* what is the name of the invention that "slices, dices, and purees your sins away?" The Wronco Forgive-o-matic.

- In *An Easter Carol,* Ebenezer Nezzer calls Seymour Schwenk, the inventor, to come to his factory. What does he want him to invent? Mechanical chickens that can lay plastic eggs.

- What crazy invention does Seymour bring with him to Nezzer's office? The Easter-ma-phonia.

NOTABLE NUMBERS IN THE BIBLE

1: One God, one Christ, and Christians are one body. Sin came into the world by one person, and we are redeemed by one person through Christ Jesus.

2: The Bible is divided into two parts, the Old Testament and the New Testament.

3: Jonah was in the belly of the fish for 3 days; Christ was raised after 3 days; and there are 3 persons in the Trinity: God, Christ, and the Holy Spirit.

5: Jesus fed 5,000 people with 5 loaves of bread *(Mark 6:44)*.

7: The number 7 is often seen in the Bible and represents an idea of perfection and completion. There are actually 107 times the number 7 is mentioned in the Bible. Here are 7 of them (and even more on the next page):
  1. God rested on the 7th day.
  2. Naaman had to dip 7 times in the Jordan.
  3. Priests and soldiers marched around Jericho 7 times on the seventh day.

4. The psalmist praised God 7 times a day *(Psalm 119:164)*.
5. Pentecost was 7 weeks after Passover.
6. It took Solomon 7 years to build the temple.
7. After the feeding of the four thousand, 7 baskets were taken up.

10: God gave Moses 10 commandments that were written on stone tablets.

12: The number 12 is a symbol for the fullness of Israel: 12 sons of Jacob; 12 tribes; 12 judges in the Book of Judges; 12 apostles; 12 gates into heaven; at age 12 Jewish boys were thought to be men.

30: At age 30, Jewish men began spiritual leadership; Jesus began his ministry at age 30.

40: The number 40 often means God is about to bring in something new—flood lasted 40 days; spies explored Canaan for 40 days; Jonah warned Nineveh for 40 days; and Jesus fasted in the wilderness for 40 days.

Seven Times Seven Times Seven!

Lots of 7s in the Bible! Here are just some more . . .

- God created the world in 7 days.
- There are 7 continents on the earth.

- There are 7 seas.
- The Book of Revelation is addressed to the 7 churches in Asia.
- Joshua was told by God to have 7 priests carry trumpets of rams' horns and march around the city 7 times on the seventh day.
- When Elisha raised a boy from the dead, he opened his eyes and sneezed 7 times.

Veggie Fun!

I've Got Your Number!

- In the show *Rack, Shack and Benny*, how many chocolate bunnies does the Nezzer Chocolate Factory make per day? 14,638. That's a lot of chocolate bunnies!

- How much money does the Milk Money Bandit ask Percy Pea for in the show *LarryBoy and the Rumor Weed*? $1.28.

- Three seems to be the magic number for Scallion bad guys. Can you name the shows in which this trio of Scallions appears? They are the Salesmen in *Madame Blueberry*, the Bandits in *The Story of Flibber-o-loo*, the Wisemen in *Daniel and the Lions' Den*.

WHAT'S IN A COLOR?

Various colors have been used by different Christian and various denominational churches over the years to represent a wide variety of symbolism in faith. How good are you at guessing what some of the following colors have symbolized?

- **Purple:** Purple has been traditionally associated with royalty in many cultures. Purple robes were worn by royalty and people of authority or high rank.

- **White:** White is purity, cleanliness, and innocence. Angels are typically depicted as wearing white. In most Western countries, white is the color for brides.

- **Gold:** Because gold is a precious metal, the color gold is associated with wealth and riches.

- **Red:** This color symbolizes the blood of Christ. In some cultures, red denotes purity, joy, and celebration.

- **Green:** This is a universal color that symbolizes creation, growth, health, and the environment. Green stands for life.

- **Blue:** This represents the color of the sky, so it is often symbolic of heaven. In addition, it has been considered as a symbol for the truth.

- **Gray:** This is the color of ash, which often represents repentance.

- **Black:** This color symbolizes grief and death. For a Christian, death is a time of sadness, but also of rejoicing because that person is now in heaven.

Thank Hue Very Much!

The Veggies are very colorful characters. Can you name the colors of the following items?

- LarryBoy's plungers: Red.
- LarryBoy's supersuit: Purple and Yellow.
- Goliath's boxing gloves: Dark Red.
- Larry's wind-up lobster: Blue.
- Color of the Penguin's toes in *Yodeling Veterinarian of the Alps*: Blue.
- Archie's Bow Tie: Red.

- Rack, Shack and Benny's hats: Black and White.
- Rack, Shack and Benny's ties: Red with Yellow polka dots.
- The underwear that is hanging on the clothesline in *Jonah–a VeggieTales Movie*: White with Red polka dots.
- Pa Grape's pirate hat: Blue and Gold.
- Princess Petunia is a rhubarb, but what color is she? Green.

WORDS AND EXPRESSIONS

Common Expressions— Where Did They Come From???

Did you ever wonder where that common expression you use or hear may have come from? Here's a few for you to consider:

- A thorn in the flesh
  (2 Corinthians 12:7).
- The good Lord *(2 Chronicles 30:18* KJV*).*
- Woe is me! *(Isaiah 6:5).*
- The handwriting is on the wall
  (Originates from Daniel 5).
- Can a leopard change its spots?
  (Jeremiah 13:23).
- Holier than thou *(Isaiah 65:5* KJV*).*

- A drop in the bucket
  (Isaiah 40:15).
- Like a lamb to the slaughter
  (Isaiah 53:7).
- Fire and brimstone *(Genesis 19:24* and *Revelation 21:8* KJV*).*
- Eat, drink, and be merry
  (Luke 12:19).
- Money is the root of all evil *(a misquote of 1 Timothy 6:10—the love of money is the root of all evil).*
- By the skin of our teeth
  (Job 19:20).
- A land of milk and honey
  (Exodus 3:8).

The Veggies sing about the wonders of the Promised Land.

Interesting Word Facts

- The word *Christian* is only in the Bible three times: *Acts 11:26; 26:28; 1 Peter 4:16.*

- The word *grandmother* is only in the Bible once—*2 Timothy 1:5.*

- The word *eternity* is only in the Bible three times—*Psalm 93:2; Proverbs 8:23; Ecclesiastes 3:11.*

- The word *trinity* is not mentioned in the Bible.

- The last word in the Bible is *Amen.*

- "Do not be afraid" appears in the Bible 106 times.

- What is the longest word in the Bible? Maher-Shalal-Hash-Baz *(Isaiah 8:1, 3).*

- God told Isaiah to name a baby Maher-Shalal-Hash-Baz. Try learning how to write that name!

"I am that hero!"

Veggie Fun!

Some fun and favorite Veggie phrases: Can you name the characters that said the following expressions?

- "And now it's time for Silly Songs with Larry." Silly Song Announcer.
- "Everybody's got a water buffalo." Larry the Cucumber.
- "I can see my house from here." Edmund (Junior Asparagus).

- "With great chocolate comes great responsibility." LarryBoy (Larry the Cucumber).
- "A message from the Lord." Jonah (Archibald Asparagus).
- "Move along, nothing to see here!" Fish and Chip (Jimmy and Jerry Gourd).
- "Hasta LaVista, Weedie!" LarryBoy (Larry the Cucumber).

- "I'm not a pickle. I'm a cucumber." Larry the Cucumber.
- "Stand up for what you believe in!" Rack, Shack and Benny (Bob, Larry, and Junior).
- "God is bigger than the Boogie Man." Junior Asparagus.
- "Nobody bakes my buddies!" Laura Carrot.
- "Super suction ears, away!" LarryBoy (Larry the Cucumber).

- "A thankful heart is a happy heart." Madame Blueberry.
- "I am that hero!" LarryBoy (Larry the Cucumber).

AMAZING BIBLE TRIVIA

- **Who were the two men who never died?** Enoch never died because God took him home or to heaven (*Genesis 5:18–27*). Elijah was taken up into heaven by a whirlwind (*2 Kings 2:11*).

- **What was the strangest way to break out of prison?** By singing (*Acts 16:22–40*). Paul and Silas were singing hymns to God when an earthquake shook the prison doors open.

- **What's a good way to remember how many books there are in the Bible?** Try this:
  Old (3 letters) Testament (9 letters) 3 and 9 together is 39.
  New (3 letters) Testament (9 letters) 3 x 9 = 27.
  Add 39 + 27 =

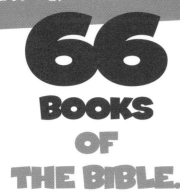

Name That Person!

- **Who was the fattest man in the Bible?** King Eglon (*Judges 3:17*).

- **Who was the strongest man in the Bible?** Samson (*Judges 14:6; 15:15; 16:1–3, 25–30*).

- **Who was the vainest man in the Bible?** Nebuchadnezzar arranged for a gold statue to be made and commanded everyone to bow down and worship it (*Daniel 3:5*).

- **Who was the fastest runner?** Asahel, who could run like a deer (*2 Samuel 2:18*).

- **Who was the shortest man in the Bible?** Zacchaeus, who climbed a sycamore tree to see Jesus (*Luke 19:3–4*).

- **What apostle traveled the most?** Paul is the most traveled (*Acts 13:4; 15:36; 18:23*).

- Who was the most beautiful woman in the Bible? Esther—she won a beauty contest to be the queen of Persia! *(Esther 2:7, 17).*

- Who was both the richest and wisest man in the Bible? Solomon *(1 Kings 3:12–13; 10:23).*

- Who was the most doubtful? Thomas, who would not believe that Jesus had risen until he could see him for himself and touch his wounds *(John 20:24–29).*

- What was the most extraordinary Bible record of a person having a different amount of fingers and toes? A man with six fingers on each hand and six toes on each foot *(2 Samuel 21:20–21).*

- Who won the very first Bible beauty contest? Abishag *(1 Kings 1:3).*

Amazing
Veggie Trivia

- Where is the Bumblyburg movie theater located? On the corner of Vischer Street and Nawrocki Road *(Larry Boy and the Rumor Weed).*

- In the show *Madame Blueberry,* as Bob, Larry, and Madame Blueberry sit in the Stuff-Mart's fast-food court, what Veggie song is playing on the speakers? "His Cheeseburger."

- In *LarryBoy and the Fib from Outer Space,* Scooter, Bumblyburg's police officer, is listening to what song in the car? "I Can Be Your Friend" from *Are You My Neighbor?*

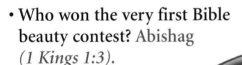

BIBLIOGRAPHY

The HOLY BIBLE, NEW INTER-NATIONAL VERSION® (NIV®). Copyright © 1973, 1978, 1984 International Bible Society. Used by permission of Zondervan. All rights reserved.

The New King James Version® (NKJV®). Copyright © 1982 by Thomas Nelson, Inc. Used by permission. All rights reserved.

King James Version (KJV). Public domain.

American Standard Version (ASV). Public domain.

The New Century Version® (NCV®). Copyright © 1987, 1988, 1991 by Thomas Nelson, Inc. Used by permission. All rights reserved.

The New Revised Standard Version® (NRSV®). Copyright © 1989, 1995 by the Division of Christian Education of the National Council of the Churches of Christ in the United States of America. Used by permission. All rights reserved.

Student's Life Application Bible, New Testament, copyright © 2005 by Tyndale House Publishers, Inc., Wheaton, IL 60189. All rights reserved.

- *Bible Humor Top Seven Lists*, Dave Veerman and Rich Anderson (Nashville: Word, 1999)

- *Young Readers Book of Bible Stories*, Helen Doss (Nashville: Abingdon, 1970)

- *Children's Bible Handbook*, Lawrence Richards (Dallas: Word, 1989)

- *The Amazing Expedition Bible*, Mary Hollingworth (Wheaton, IL: Baker, 1997)

- *The Big Book of Bible Facts*, Rhona Pipe and Graham Round (London: John Hunt Publishing, 1998)

- *A Bucket of Surprises*, J. John and Mark Stibbe (Oxford, UK: Monarch, 2002)

- *A Theological Miscellany*, T. J. McTavish (Nashville: W Publishing, 2005)

- *Somewhere Angels*, Larry Libby (Sisters, OR: Questar, 1994)

- *Angels*, Billy Graham (Dallas: Word, 1994)

- *Angels, Satan, and Demons*, Robert Lightner (Nashville: Word, 1998)

- *God*, J. Carl Laney (Nashville: Word, 1999)

- *It Couldn't Just Happen*, Lawrence Richards (Dallas: Word, 1989)

- *The New Compact Bible Dictionary*, T. Alton Bryant, ed. (Grand Rapids, MI: Zondervan, 1967)

- *Topical Index of the Bible*, Doyle D. Gilliam (New Delhi, India: Bible Teacher Publications, 1976)

- *The Bible Almanac for Kids: A Journey of Discovery into the Wild, Incredible, and Mysterious Facts & Trivia of the Bible*, Terry Hall (Lakeland, FL: White Stone Books, 2004)

- *The Student Bible Guide*, Tim Dowley (Minneapolis: Augsburg, 1996)

- *The Jesus Encyclopedia*, Lois Rock (Nashville: TommyNelson, 2005)

- *The MacArthur Topical Bible*, John MacArthur (Nashville: W Publishing, 1999)

- *Children's Encyclopedia*, David Hancock (London: Usborne Publishing Limited, 2002)

- *The Everything Kids Bible Trivia Book*, Kathi Wager and Aubrey Wagner (Cincinnati: F & W Publications, Inc., 2004)

- *Guinness World Records 2005* (London: Hit Entertainment/Guinness World Records Limited, 2004)

- *How the Bible Came to Us*, Meryl Doney (Oxford: Lion Publishing, 1985)

- *International Children's Bible Dictionary*, Lynn Waller (Nashville: Word Publishing 1989)

- *Where to Find It in the Bible – The Ultimate A to Z Resource*, Ken Anderson (Nashville: Thomas Nelson Publishers, 1996)

- *World Almanac for Kids 2006* (New York: World Almanac Education Group, Inc., 2005)

- *Young's Analytical Concordance to the Bible* (Peabody: Hendrickson Publishers, 1984)

www.caltech.edu

www.nasa.gov

www.harvard.edu

www.usgs.gov

www.stanford.edu

www.britannica.com

http://columbia.thefreedictionary.com

www.state.nj.us/labor

www.overpopulation.org

www.bibleplaces.com

www.pbs.org